DON'T WASTE THIS STORM

*Hope-Filled Thriving, Not Just Barely
Surviving, in the Storms of Life*

ROD KNOERR

WESTBOW
PRESS®
A DIVISION OF THOMAS NELSON
& ZONDERVAN

WestBow Press books may be ordered through booksellers or by contacting:

WestBow Press
A Division of Thomas Nelson & Zondervan
1663 Liberty Drive
Bloomington, IN 47403
www.westbowpress.com
844-714-3454

ISBN: 978-1-6642-5807-5 (sc)
ISBN: 978-1-6642-5806-8 (e)

Print information available on the last page.

WestBow Press rev. date: 2/25/2022

DEDICATION

This book is dedicated to every person, couple, or family who finds themselves in a storm of life where they can't seem to see up from down. Your storm may be health related, financial, relational, or even the loss of a loved one. No matter what the nature of your storm may be, a storm is a storm and they can literally suck the life out of you.

As you join my wife Beth and me on this very real and transparent story of our life storm experience, it is my hope that you will gain insights and tools that will allow you to not just live as a victim in the storm waiting for it to pass, but will instead truly live courageously with purpose and hope in the midst of the storm!

CONTENTS

CHAPTER 1

Where It All Started

It was an ordinary Friday night in March 1977. I was in my second semester of college, attending a local state college in Michigan and living at home with my parents. I was a psychology major thinking about going to grad school for clinical psychology or possibly medical school. I knew that I wanted to help people.

My best friend from high school was attending the University of Michigan, but he had a friend who he felt was shy, and he wanted me to take him out to one of the clubs. We went to the Eleventh Frame Lounge, which was basically a bar hooked to a bowling alley that had music playing and a dance floor.

This friend of my high school friend was super shy. He had never been on a date. After a couple glasses of beers, I hoped his inhibitions were reduced, and I encouraged him to go to a table with two young ladies and ask one of them to dance. He finally got up the courage to go over and ask one of them to dance. I could tell by her body language that he was gently turned down. So much for me building up his self-esteem.

About a half hour later, for some reason I decided to go over and ask the same girl to dance. She said yes! With disco music blaring (it was the late '70s), I found out that she and her friend were dental hygiene students. We danced a couple of dances and talked a little before heading back to our tables.

I didn't have the guts to invite her to my table or to go over by her table. I did get her name. But not being all that bold, I didn't get her phone number. I did learn what street she lived on. To this day, almost forty-five years later, I can still see that red blouse, blue slacks, and those unbelievable, alive green eyes!

All the way home, this guy and I kept repeating her name and street name. I didn't want to forget. Beth Fritzler … Colon St. Beth Fritzler … Colon St. Beth Fritzler … Colon St. If her phone number was unlisted, I was determined to knock on every door on Colon St. to find her.

When I got home, for some reason my mom was awake. I told my mom two things that night. "I met a girl with the prettiest green eyes, and I think I could marry her!" Well, her number wasn't unlisted, and Colon St., which was really spelled Kollen St., was only two blocks long.

I called Beth the next day and asked her out on a date. I found out that she attended a college about forty-five minutes south of where we lived from Monday through Friday and lived with her grandparents during the week. She then came home on weekends. So that meant I had to wait almost a week to see those beautiful green eyes.

On our first date, I took her out to dinner, and we quickly discovered that our Christian faith was important to both of us. Beth was a Sunday school teacher, and I had always been very involved with our youth program at my church. We belonged to the same denomination, and by the second date, we were going to church together. When I look back, I am amazed. Before Beth and I had decided to date each other exclusively, we were going to church together.

After a few dates, I really knew that Beth could be the one! I did have one big concern. On the night I met Beth, in our limited conversation, I found out she had graduated from high school a year before me. She was actually two years older than me.

I kind of fibbed to Beth on that loud, music-blaring dance floor and said I was in my third year of college. When you are eighteen, it feels much younger than twenty. I was afraid she might not be interested in dating a kid who was eighteen.

On our third date, I decided I had to come clean. I don't remember the words I used, but I was so worried about what Beth would think of me for not being truthful the first time we met. I was so worried this mature, grace-filled twenty-year-old with sparkling green eyes would not have given me the time of day if she had known I was only eighteen. As I stumbled over my words and tried to be truthful and apologize, Beth didn't say a word.

There was this long pause before she looked at me with a big smile on her face and said the words I will never forget, "What's the big deal? My mom is two years older than my dad!" I guess in the time we'd known each other she saw a maturity and love for the Lord that she was intrigued with. Years later, I also heard it was my blue eyes and blond hair.

For the next two months of April and May, we dated on weekends when she was back home from school. We began to meet each other's families. I even went to Flint and got to meet Beth's mom's side of the family. Beth's mom had five sisters and one brother. That was a great day because I came to find out they all were very involved in their churches, and the Lord was at the centers of their families.

My first year of college had ended, and Beth had completed her first year of dental hygiene school and was living at home for the summer. We went out on a date, and as I was dropping her off and saying good night, I was hit with probably the most unexpected tidal wave of my life. Beth let me know that she often went up north to her grandma's cottage in the summer. There was a guy a lot older than me who she often saw when she was with her grandma. She told me she just wasn't sure about us and in essence broke up with me.

I was totally blindsided. I was positive she was the one! I would like to say that I turned it all over to the Lord in prayer and trusted that he had me in his hands. Unfortunately, I threw a summerlong pity party! The drinking age was eighteen in Michigan at that time.

I went to the clubs on weekends and, I am sure, had too many beers to drink. Thank goodness God was looking over me as I drove home each night. I had never felt such intense hurt at the depth of my being. I couldn't live without those green eyes that sparkled with life!

In September, I started my second year of undergrad and was working at a farm and garden store. Beth's parents were really into feeding birds in their backyard. The place I worked at sold thistle seed. Beth's parents fed the finches with this and it was hard to find. I decided to stop over and take them some thistle seed once Beth was away at hygiene school.

I knocked on their door, with no intent of staying or visiting. They invited me in and wouldn't take no for an answer. Then they offered me a cold iced tea. No matter what I did, they were intent on me staying for a while. Little did I know Beth was not at school yet. She was in the garage refinishing a piece of antique furniture. Her parents were stalling until they could get Beth in the house. What a surprise for both Beth and me as she entered the living room. We visited a bit, and I said I would call her.

A few weeks later, we went out on a date for the first time in almost four months. I had started to date a young lady a few times in September. She was a great person, she loved the Lord, and we seemed to have a lot in common. When I made the date with Beth before even knowing if we would get back together, I told this girl that I had met Beth a few months ago and we'd broken up and that I could not date her if there was any chance of getting back with Beth. I am sure she felt just like I did when Beth broke up with me.

Well, the night of the date came up, and I was gonna make it memorable. It was the week of Halloween. The area where we lived in Michigan was referred to as the Tri-Cities— Bay City, Saginaw, and Midland. That night I took Beth to a fall harvest fest in Saginaw, to dinner in Bay City, dancing in Midland, and then home to Saginaw. We decided then that we would date exclusively, and by Beth's birthday the week before Christmas, I gave her a sapphire ring. Back then, a sapphire was like a promise ring prior to an engagement ring.

In January, I tried to introduce Beth to downhill snow skiing. I had taken up skiing the winter before I met Beth. After a day on a ski hill, it was evident that Beth was not going to be a downhill skier. Beth was just not courageous enough for the sport!

We were in their family room after a day at the ski hill. Beth and I were talking about the future. By now I had decided to change my major to pre-medicine, which meant I had probably eight more years of college. Beth had this gentle spirit that wasn't loud or over the top. As I reflect on the conversation years later, I claim that Beth, in her subtle, suggestive way, asked me to ask her to marry me!

As we were talking about how many more years of college I had, Beth said, "Then you probably won't want to get married till after you are out of school." Even though Beth and I had not talked about this subject, we both wanted to honor the Lord and to be sexually pure until we married. When Beth mentioned waiting till after medical school to get married, all I could think of was how beautiful she was and how attracted I was to her and that there was no way I could possibly make it eight more years.

The next thing out of my mouth was "Beth will you marry me?" Those beautiful green eyes, those beautiful green eyes. She said *Yes*! At the age of nineteen, after a total of less than six months of dating, we were engaged. I remember going to the jewelry store and picking out a diamond ring. I was putting myself through college and that $400 for a ring seemed like so much money back then.

On Valentine's Day I gave Beth her diamond ring. A year later, on May 12, we would be husband and wife. The pastor's message for our wedding ceremony was based on Numbers 6:24–26, "The Lord bless you and keep you, the Lord make his face shine upon you and be gracious to you; the Lord turn His face toward you and give you peace!" Our faith was the foundation for our marriage and for our eventual family.

Jesus says in Matthew 7:24–27, "Therefore everyone who hears these words of mine and puts them into practice is like a wise man who built his house on the rock. The rain came down, the streams rose, and the winds blew and beat against the house; yet it did not fall, because it had its foundation on the rock. But everyone who hears these words of mine and does not put them into practice is like a foolish man who built his house on sand. The rain came down, the streams rose, and the winds blew and beat against that house, and it fell with a great crash."

Within days of meeting Beth, we worshipped together. We committed to build our dating, marriage, and future family on the *rock*. Little did we know how fierce the winds and storms of life would be in the years ahead, but we knew we were secure on the rock!

REFUGE REFLECTIONS

1. What does it mean to build on the "rock" as an individual, as a couple, as a family?

2. What areas of your life are built on sand?

3. Reflect on this thought, "It doesn't matter how hard you try or how intense you pray when you build on the sand!

4. When you or anyone you know is looking for a future spouse, run to the Lord and look to the right and look to the left. The one running to the Lord to your right or life is also seeking to build on the rock!

CHAPTER 2

Storms That Blow Us Off or On Course

After getting married we rented a house near my parents as I finished my last year of undergraduate studies at Saginaw Valley State University. We headed off to Ann Arbor in the fall of 1980 to begin dental school at the University of Michigan.

The course Beth and I had charted was to graduate from dental school, return to the Bay City/Saginaw area and have a dental practice near our parents. We also wanted a big family and dreamed of possibly five children. Having a large family was not in our backgrounds. Beth had one brother and I only had a younger brother and sister.

When we arrived in Ann Arbor, we lived in married housing on the North Campus very near Concordia College which is a Lutheran undergraduate college. I grew up going to a little country Lutheran Church and school. Beginning in eighth grade and continuing into high school, I sometimes wondered if God wanted me to be a pastor. My parents hadn't gone to college and most of my relatives were farmers or factory workers. I decided I wanted to help people, so I was going to be a dentist.

Living so close to this college made me question if I was on the course that God wanted me on until I met a professor who belonged to the church we worshipped at during our time in Ann Arbor. He was very active in our church and he led a Bible study at the dental school. I felt that was a sign that God wanted me to be a dentist and be active in my faith as a layperson, not as a pastor.

Beth worked as a dental hygienist while I was very busy the first two years of dental school. We decided if we wanted a big family, we would start our family during dental school. Our first child, Rod II, was born in the summer before my third year.

Because I was putting myself through school, I delivered 7-Up in the Detroit area in the summer. Just days before Rod was born, I came out to my delivery truck and two individuals held me up. I had a 38-caliber pistol aimed at my forehead. For some reason, they did not pull the trigger. God was truly looking over me. Another driver, who had three children, was shot but he returned to work a few months later because he needed to provide for his family. I was motivated to do well in dental school.

At the beginning of my last year of dental school, we welcomed our daughter Kari into the world. The last year of dental school went fast, especially with two small children. We were then moving back to Saginaw near Beth's parents. I would rent space from Beth's family dentist and start my dental practice, while working part-time for my family dentist in Bay City.

The first five years after dental school were professionally very satisfying, I purchased the dental practices of two retiring dentists who were located across the street from each other. My staff and I made sure that our patients knew that they were not just a number. When you treat people with the love of Jesus, they in turn refer their friends and relatives. Five years out of dental school, at the age of thirty, I built a new dental building! To friends, family, and patients we were a real success story.

During those five years, Beth and I, as a husband and wife and as parents, experienced the complete range from pure joy to paralyzing crises. Shortly before buying the second dental practice our daughter Kristi was born. She was such a beautiful baby with the longest dark hair at birth. Beth and I felt so blessed, three healthy, beautiful children in a little over three years.

The day after Kristi came home from the hospital, I had decided to take the day off from work. This was the only time I had ever taken time off because Beth's mom lived nearby and was always there to help. God knew why I took off that day. Midmorning, Beth had nursed Kristi and had laid her down and walked across the room to get a diaper. When she went to pick her up, she had stopped breathing and was turning blue.

I will never forget Beth's panic-filled scream. I took Kristi in my arms and was about to administer CPR, when our three-year-old son asked, "Is our baby gonna die?" After a few short CPR breaths our baby started breathing. We decided that it was quicker for Beth to drive me to the hospital, and I would administer CPR if she needed it.

Kristi was a classic sudden infant death syndrome (SIDS) baby! If it had happened at night, we would have lost our new baby. Kristi had to wear a fetal heart monitor for the next six months. She never stopped breathing again. I have taken biannual CPR classes for the last forty years and have only given CPR one time. God knew I should take the day off work that day.

A year after Kristi was born our son, Rod, started kindergarten. The principal of Rod's school was a patient of mine. I was seeing my first patient when the school principal called and in his monotone voice he said, "Your son has been run over and your wife is quite upset!" I broke the speed limit driving to the school a few miles away.

Apparently when Beth was dropping Rod off by the school door, she was looking toward the passenger side and didn't realize Rod had crossed in front of the car. Beth had run over her own son. Rod was directly in front of the car, so the tires did not run over him. If his head had not turned his skull would have been crushed by the frame of our station wagon. He only had facial abrasions. In the course of a year, two of our children could have died.

Fast forward two years to 1989. We celebrated our tenth

anniversary in May as we were breaking ground on the dental building. In July, after Beth's first miscarriage, Knoerr baby number four, Reid, was born! Talk about busy times—four beautiful children age seven and under, practicing dentistry, and going through the logistics of working with a contractor to build an office building.

During this season, I served in various roles in our local church. I was a member of the choir and Beth and I were in Bible studies and were starting to make friends with other parents of young children. We were definitely enjoying living near both sets of parents. Life was super busy with good stuff.

Because I was a blue-collar country boy at heart, I saved us a lot of money by staining and finishing all exterior and interior woodwork of the soon-to-be-completed dental building. This was a very time-consuming job. Thank goodness my dear father-in-law helped. At this point in my life, I thought I could burn the candle at both ends and not get burned. We moved into the building the beginning of October and two days later headed up to my parent's cottage in northern Michigan. I was an avid bow and arrow deer hunter!

I told Beth that I was too tired to drive and asked her to drive. A few miles from the exit where she was going to drop me off in the woods to hunt, Beth told me she was tired and asked me to drive. We stopped on the side of the expressway and Beth nursed Reid and put him in his car seat and I took the wheel.

Within a mile of taking the wheel, I had dozed and was off the road in the median, clipping the pine tree branches. I was in the process at 65 mph of slowly returning to the road when a tire blew, and our van began to roll. After the third roll, we miraculously landed on the tires. As I got everyone out of the van, we found out Rod had a severely cut finger that would require stitches. After nursing Reid, Beth had put him in the car seat without buckling him in. He had come out of the seat when we rolled and now he wouldn't stop crying.

A car stopped and took Beth and the kids to the local clinic. It was determined to fly Reid by helicopter to our hometown hospital in Saginaw. Reid did indeed have a fractured skull. He ended up requiring no treatment and today he is a happily married father of three. This was our third child in a three-year period to truly have a near death experience.

Every weekend that we vacationed at my parent's cottage, you would read in the newspaper about car accidents with fatalities. God was gracious to our family. We had a fully loaded old time Coleman metal cooler that was flying around in the van when we were rolling. Not one of my four sweet children had their skull crushed by it. When our van quit rolling and I was getting my family out of the van and checking each one of them, I said to them, "God really must want to use our family in the future!"

The thought of God wanting me in ministry came back at that time. I wondered if God was using the van accident like a big 2 x 4 to get my attention. Over the next two years God really allowed my dental practice to thrive in the new building and location. We were doing so well that we decided to build a house in a newer subdivision close to my dental office. We moved into the new house in the fall of 1991. Even though I continued to feel a void in my life, the thought of going into ministry got drowned out with the busyness of four children and the dental practice.

As the year 1992 began, Beth and I had so much to be thankful for—our four beautiful children, our parents who lived nearby, and our church family! At thirty-three years of age my dental practice was at a place where I should have been so blessed and content, yet I felt a void inside.

I was in church one Sunday when our pastor was reading from the letter to the Romans when a verse just grabbed me. Romans 10:14 states, "How, then can they call on the one they have not believed in? And how can they believe in the one whom they have not heard? And how can they hear without someone preaching to them?" The days following that church service I could not get that verse out of my mind! Did God really want to use me to bring others to faith?

At different points in our marriage when I felt that heart tugging to ministry, I had talked with Beth about it. This time as Beth and I talked I could tell that she knew that this time something was different. I called our denomination seminary and received information about attending seminary. It was a three-year academic process with an additional internship year in a church.

I had a patient who changed careers and was now a pastor. I took him out to lunch and asked him how he knew that God was calling him into the pastoral ministry. I just wasn't sure I was worthy of such a calling. He told me he asked his pastor the same question and his answer was, "When that tugging at your heart doesn't go away!" Since about eighth grade I had periodically felt this call to the ministry. I guess twenty years qualifies for "when it doesn't go away!"

I will never forget the conversation Beth and I had after I met with my patient. We were living the dream we had as a couple way back when we were dating. We were living near our parents. Beth and her mom were like best friends. We had four beautiful kids, we were very active in our church, and our children were beginning to attend our church school. My dental practice was doing very well.

I will never forget what my grace-filled, God-loving wife said to me with tears streaming down her face, "I love living in Saginaw near mom and dad, but you have to listen to God and do what he is telling you to do!" I know in the letter to the Ephesians it says the husband is the head of the house. Up until now, even in the years following, this was the *only* time I made a major decision where Beth and I were not in agreement!

Within a few weeks, my practice was put up for sale and by midsummer we were saying goodbye to patients, friends, and relatives and we were moving to Fort Wayne, Indiana. I decided to enroll at the Fort Wayne Seminary because it was only three hours from family compared to the seminary in St. Louis. I was enrolled in an intensive ten credit Greek class and we were unpacking and getting our children ready to start school in Indiana! Obviously moving our children into a new state and new schools were a concern to Beth and me as parents, but we trusted the Lord.

I decided to take a heavy class load so that I could complete my academics and internship in three years instead of four. Because I wasn't working, I had time after school to be involved with my children's school. God blessed our family with our fifth child, Christian, while we were in Fort Wayne. The seminary I attended catered to second career students with families. We made so many good friends during this time. This educational interlude in my work career was such a blessing on so many levels.

My internship year would be back in Michigan, but it would not start until November. I moved Beth and the kids to Holland, Michigan, in August so our children could start school in September. I lived in the dormitory at seminary to complete my last semester and traveled to Holland every weekend. My internship year was in a mission church where we worshipped on Sundays in an elementary school gymnasium.

In some cases, the seminary intern ends up staying at the internship church and becomes their pastor. That was not the case for our family. My sister's church in Clarkston, on the east side of Michigan, was looking for an assistant pastor for youth and family ministry. After many interviews and much prayer, I was selected as their assistant pastor. So, after a year in Holland, we moved our family for the third time in a little over three years. New schools again for the kids!

I was ordained into the pastoral ministry in December 1995. The verse that was read at my ordination service was Isaiah 40:31, "But those who hope in the Lord will renew their strength. They will soar on wings like eagles; they will run and not grow weary, they will walk and not be faint." The pastor who ordained me during his sermon looked at me and said, "Brother Rod, you will be tested, you will be refined in the fire!" Little did I know what he was talking about!

Over the next six years I would serve in three churches. This was during the Promise Keepers men's ministry years. At my internship church I started a men's ministry and took a group of men to a Promise Keepers stadium event. When I started my role as assistant pastor of church with about 300 worshippers, I had a goal to take fifty men to a Promise Keepers event.

The senior pastor was concerned because the church treasurer had to pay for the tickets in advance. We indeed sold all the tickets. Fifty men attended! We then started a weekly men's ministry called Men of Faith. The next year I had an outrageous goal of selling one hundred tickets. I am optimistic! Looking back, I must have been out of my mind. We sold ninety-eight tickets and donated the other two.

After two and a half years in Clarkston, one of my old patients had retired and moved to Illinois. The church he belonged to was looking for a new pastor, so he mentioned my name. After much prayer I decided to become the lead pastor at this church in Illinois. Another move for our beautiful family. I know moving the kids into their fourth new school in six years was really weighing on Beth. Beth had been homeschooling our youngest two sons so the transition really affected our oldest three, with two now in high school.

After about nine months at this church, it was evident that my vision for ministry was not aligned with this church. After many meetings and much prayer, in February I asked for my peaceful release as their pastor. Beth and I were praying on if we should move back to Michigan or finish out the school year with the kids.

A group of people from the church I left approached me and ask if I would help them start a church in the same town as the church I served. I remember telling Beth if I got involved with this group, the next church I would be serving in this denomination would be in Siberia. It was not a politically correct move, but my heart was drawn to helping these dear people.

I decided to meet with the district president who was over all the churches of our denomination in Northern Illinois. He did not tell me not to help start the church. He told me that the new church would receive no funding from the denomination. A meeting was arranged with people who were interested in starting a new church. At that meeting I asked everyone to put the amount they could tithe each month in support of the new church into a hat. Understand, I had five children and my wife was a stay-at-home mom.

I totaled the amount that these dear people were willing to tithe, and my response was, "Let's go!" My vision for the new church could be summed up in four words, cell groups and celebrative worship. This new church would transition to contemporary worship, and we would have a foundation of small groups where people and youth could relationally connect.

Little did I know when I was serving my seminary internship year in a mission church that worshipped in an elementary school gymnasium, that five years later God would use my experience to start a new church. Within days of the planning meeting, we signed a contract to rent the use of a local elementary school gymnasium and cafeteria on Sunday mornings.

We decided the first two services would be on Good Friday and Easter. When we were considering how to do the worship services, we borrowed a sound system and found people to sing on a worship team. The elementary school had an old piano we could use.

We now needed someone to play the piano to accompany our worship. On Good Friday a fifteen-year-old girl was on the piano bench. On Easter Sunday, with almost two hundred people filling the gymnasium, a thirteen-year-old girl, who had gone a year since her last piano lesson, played the piano. The two young ladies that God used were my daughters, Kari and Kristi. I have never been prouder as a dad!

There is nothing that compares to the joy, the passion, and the close fellowship of the experience of starting a new church. Within a year we added a full-time person to work with the children and youth. We were able to purchase property to build a church. As good as things were going at this church, there was an awkwardness with some of the people from the church I had resigned from.

After much prayer and discussion with Beth, we began to feel God had wanted to use us to start this church, but he had someone else in mind to take it into the future. In addition, our parents in Michigan were beginning to get up in age. We could be much more help to our parents in Michigan. I contacted the district president's office and asked if my name could be put out for a church in Michigan.

After two years of waiting and three years after being used by God to start the church, I approached the leaders of our church and explained how Beth and I felt. I asked for my peaceful release and within a few months we moved back to Michigan. There was a range of emotions from the people of this church ranging from anger to hurt and disappointment. But to this day I know it was what God wanted and it was what was best for this young church!

While trying to arrange a meeting with our denomination district president in Michigan, I took the appropriate continuing education classes and became relicensed as a dentist. Beth worked part time as a dental hygienist while I was waiting to start a dental job. We rented a house in the town where my younger sister lived.

When I finally met with the district president, he informed me that my name was never circulated for a pastoral position in Michigan. We decided after a ten-year break from dentistry that I would go back to working as a dentist and see how God could use my ministry experience as a layperson.

During those years God began to teach me that I was Rod, not God. When you are way too busy doing way too many good things, it is not a good way to live. As a result, I was often impatient and had a short fuse. I was blessed to be used by God to start a men's ministry in every church I served. If men are to be the spiritual leaders in their families, they need to rely on and support their brothers in the faith!

In each church I served, I began relational small group ministries. I raised up small group leaders for Junior High and Senior High

Youth. Beth and I felt if we had a need for community, others must also have the same need. In all four churches we served, we definitely encouraged and expanded small group men's, women's, and couple's ministries. Satan knew that when God's people grow closer to each other in community they grow stronger in the faith and in their marriages.

As we were preparing to leave full-time ministry, I told Beth that she was a far better pastor's wife than I was a pastor. So many of my seminary classmates had very outgoing, opinionated wives that I knew would create conflict when they were serving a church. My gentle, grace-filled wife never sought the limelight. She was quite happy serving under the radar, allowing others to receive the praise.

In every church I served Beth was involved with starting or serving in a women's ministry. Beth used our home to host youth small groups. Beth often hosted women's gatherings at our home. In the second church I served, Beth worked with the leaders of the Mothers of Preschoolers (MOPS) group. Beth was the perfect person to be involved with them. She had a preschooler at the time along with the experience of mothering four older children.

In each church we were at Beth started an annual tradition called Advent by Candlelight. Beth would plan an Advent women's dinner where she found women to host a table of eight. These women would ornately decorate their tables and bring their own table service and invite women. This was an annual fancy night out for the women of these churches!

Beth's quiet personality made her an amazing small group leader. She was so good at encouraging others in the small group to open up and share. So many people were blessed by her quiet, gentle leadership. Beth didn't see herself as a leader, just a humble servant of the Lord.

Due to Beth's strong faith and reliance on the Lord, she was able to not just weather this season in full-time ministry as a wife and mother, but to grow as a woman of faith and as a humble servant of the Lord. When we got married Beth and I never could have imagined the impact God would make through her gentle humble spirit!

We found during our time in full-time church work that the words of Matthew 6:21, "For where your treasure is, there your heart will be too," and Matthew 6:33, "But seek first the kingdom of God and His righteousness, and all these things will be given to you as well," were true. Our lessons, growth, and blessings were not what we expected. But when we stayed focused on Jesus and serving him, we were blessed as a family in ways we could never have imagined.

When we moved back to Michigan and left full-time church work, I am sure many of our friends and relatives saw our time in ministry as a mistake or a failure. That would be Satan talking. Much can be learned from these stormy detours in life.

Our children attended school in six different cities in ten years. They were definitely in the public eye as PK's (pastor's kids)! As adults, each one of my children are very comfortable in large group settings and are very relational due to those years. In the almost twenty years since leaving full-time ministry, there has been so many moments where Beth and I could see the fruit that was bore through our efforts. Through what many perceived as a mistake on our part, God lovingly and strategically was preparing us and our children to serve him more fully in the years ahead.

REFUGE REFLECTIONS

1. Think of a time in your life when you took a leap of faith for the Lord, and it didn't go as you had planned.

2. Following the Lord is about trust. Where in your life is God calling you to take up your cross and follow him, no matter the consequences?

3. When things come crashing down are you still able to see how God used you for his purposes and how you grew stronger in your faith due to that season?

CHAPTER 3

Shifting Winds of Transition

When we returned to Michigan after leaving full-time ministry, I worked as an associate dentist in various offices. In 2005 and 2006 we repeated history and purchased the dental practices of two retiring dentists in Flushing.

I woke up on my fiftieth birthday in September 2008, rolled over and said to Beth, "I want to live closer to our two new grandbabies!" Our oldest grandchild, Calvin, was eight months old and living five hours away in southern Wisconsin and our granddaughter Lexi was two months old and living about two hours away in Marshall, Michigan. To the woman who was born to be a mother of five and a grandmother, Beth was all ears!

After some lively discussion and prayer, we decided to make an offer to purchase a dental practice near Marshall. We would then be living near little Lexi, my daughter Kari, and her husband Zach. We would also now be two hours closer to little Calvin, my daughter Kristi, and her husband Jon. Because of the downturn in the housing market, we made an offer on a house on a lake. We had always owned a boat and we hoped living on a lake would allow us to share our love for water sports with our grandchildren!

Well, wouldn't you know it, the dental practice purchase didn't end up working out. After much prayer we decided to take a leap of faith and buy the house and move to Marshall. I now began making an almost two hour commute to my office in Flushing. Shortly after moving to Marshall in May 2009, General Motors filed for bankruptcy. Understand, a good percentage of my patients were General Motors retirees. With the bankruptcy, they lost their dental insurance.

You want to talk about a storm slamming you. I was still paying off the two practices and now this. Well, I remember meeting with our staff and saying to them, "We are not going to barely survive, we are going to thrive!" I had no clue how I was going to do that at the time. I told Beth there was a good chance we could go bankrupt.

I then got creative. We dropped my weekly practice schedule down to only three days, Monday–Wednesday. This allowed me to get a job working as an associate dentist on Thursdays and Fridays near where we lived in Marshall. Beth got a part-time job as a dental hygienist near Marshall. The Lord was providing!

This began a schedule of driving to Flushing Monday mornings and driving back at the end of the day so I could see my youngest son's tennis and lacrosse matches on Mondays. I would then drive to Flushing Tuesday mornings and stay overnight Tuesday, then drive home on Wednesday at the end of the day. After two years of doing this Beth quit her job and she started working with me in our dental office in Flushing.

So often people when caught in the storms of life spend all their time looking at what they don't have or what shouldn't have happened. Those weird four years of commuting and sleeping on a blow-up bed at the dental office one night a week were filled with so many blessings.

Living in Marshall was such a blessing to Beth and me. Two days a week my daughter Kari worked as a dental hygienist. She would drop little Lexi off just before bedtime the day before she worked and Beth would babysit her on Mondays, the day I went to Flushing by myself. Also, our daughter Kristi and her family ended up moving to northern Indiana and they then lived a little over an hour away.

Beth and I truly had the best dental team you could ever dream of. Beth did not work as a dental hygienist while we were bringing up our five children. She started working part time when our youngest son was in junior high.

For the first time Beth and I worked together in our dental office for two years. It was so much fun! We would go out to eat every Tuesday night when we stayed overnight. All those years of bringing up our five beautiful children, for two days it was just Beth and me, with no children or grandchildren to take our attention off each other.

In January 2013, it was hard to believe that what was at the time in 2009 seen as a short-term answer to the economic crisis had turned into almost four years of commuting to Flushing. After much prayer Beth and I decided to sell the dental practice. We just felt God had a new plan for us closer to Marshall. At the end of March 2013, we signed the papers to sell our dental practice!

Shortly after selling our dental practice, Beth and I headed to Florida for a relaxing vacation together. On the way back to Michigan, Beth and I visited the Smoky Mountains. It was such a magical visit. We had spent our honeymoon in Gatlinburg thirty-four years earlier in 1979.

Coming back to Michigan I just wanted to relax and spend time with Beth. Eventually I would find a dental associate position. Beth and I had started a daily reading plan that would lead us to read through the entire Bible in a year. Every morning we sat on our couch and we each read the Bible and had devotion time. It seemed like I had been busy, busy, busy, on the move since my teenage years. For the first time in my adult life, I had space to relax and breathe!

The Beth and I time was short-lived. My mom had passed away suddenly the previous October and my dad did not feel he could live alone in Florida, so his house was put up for sale and he moved in with my sister Vicki and her husband Scott. After six months of living with them, my sister and Scott needed a break. Beth and I offered to have Dad move in with us for a while toward the end of April.

When Dad moved in with us, my sister and Dad seemed to think at age seventy-five he needed to live in an assisted-living facility. We lived on a lake, and I felt that Dad was a little depressed. He had one of those adult tricycle bikes in Florida. I suggested that it may be good for him to get some physical exercise.

He initially told me no. One day I got my bike and the tricycle bike out and asked if he could start by riding a few houses down the road. Each day we rode a little farther. Within a week he was riding about a half mile and back. Within two months Dad, on his own, rode the two miles around our lake!

I was sure my dad could take care of himself at age seventy-five and live on his own. I actually started checking out options for him to move into an apartment complex where he would stay in the summers when he came back to Michigan from Florida. My sister and brother weren't sure, so my brother Todd and his wife Sherry had Dad move in with them. After a month or so, he also agreed Dad could be independent. My dad indeed moved into a seniors' apartment complex for a couple of years before he needed assisted living.

So often when families are faced with making decisions about their older parents, siblings end up fighting and often families are estranged over making decisions about parents. The opposite happened with my siblings. We actually began to appreciate each other more through the process. Thankfully we all were praying and looking to the Lord for guidance and the Lord did not disappoint! I discovered if you pray first, you often don't open your mouth!

As I was interviewing for possible dental associate positions, Beth and I were really enjoying the simple things like waking up together, doing our devotion time together on the couch looking at the beauty of the lake and the sun rise over the lake. During one of these mornings I asked Beth, "remember that Dr. McKinley?" She answered, "Who?" I then told her that he was the dentist who stood up and was recruiting for a medical/dental mission trip to Romania when we visited Family Bible Church a year before.

For the first time in my adult life, I had space in my life to consider going on a mission trip. We were running errands in Battle Creek, and I told Beth as we drove by his office that we should stop in on the way home and inquire about this mission trip. What happened next was truly a "God moment." On the way back home from our errand we were heading to Dr. McKinley's office, and I told Beth, "Let's stop at Subway for lunch." We walked into Subway and who do you think is the person in line ahead of us, Dr. McKinley!

I found out the mission trip was in the middle of July, about a week after my daughter Kari was due with our grandson Liam. Beth was afraid I would miss the birth. I decided to commit to the mission team as a dentist. About a week later a church where I had been substitute preaching approached me to be an adult chaperone for a Youth Ministry gathering in San Antonio. This trip was the week before the Fourth of July. After a lot of discussion and prayer, I decided to go as a chaperone on the youth trip and wait till next year to go to Romania.

I emailed Dr. McKinley on a Saturday night, informing him of my decision to not go on the mission trip. The next morning at church our senior pastor preached a sermon about following the Spirit's leading. He was trying to make the point that often when God is leading us to do something we are looking for every reason to say no. He said, "When you feel the nudge of the Spirit to do something, don't say I will think about it, I'm not sure, next year, just say yes!"

I have never felt God directly talking to me like at that moment. Dr. McKinley usually worshipped in our early service, but today he was at the same service we attended. At the end of our worship, I walked up to him and said, "Disregard the email I sent you." He looked at me and said, "What email?" He hadn't checked his emails yet! I was really going to Romania in July!

My dad was living with us and moved out right about the time I headed to San Antonio for the mega youth gathering. It was an awesome, busy week with the youth. Shortly after I got back from

San Antonio, little Liam Zachary was born to my daughter Kari and her husband Zach. I didn't miss the birth. He entered this world in the window between when I was in San Antonio and before I left for Romania.

I was so excited to be a part of this Romanian mission team. To be able to use my dental gifts on the mission field. I was now counting down the days after Liam's birth until we would leave for Romania. God truly wanted me in Romania … but his purposes were a little different than I expected!

REFUGE REFLECTIONS

My two siblings and our spouses grew closer together and more in agreement during the year following the passing of our mom as we tried to decide on how independent our father could live. Why? So many families are split and end up divided going through the similar decisions related to elder care. As I reflect on the process I came to a few realizations.

1. None of us had any ulterior motives. We all saw our dad's estate as "his" money, not as our future inheritance. Any decisions that would be made were for his best interests, period!

2. We at first had very differing opinions. We sought out professional counsel! As my dad regularly met with a counselor, the professional advice and counsel really helped as we tried to consider each other's differing opinions.

3. We each had a chance to have Dad live with us. There are things you just won't understand until you experience it. We began to understand each other better.

4. In James 1:19 it says, "Everyone should be quick to listen, slow to speak, and slow to become angry!" I know for me this was key. Instead of reacting and giving an opinion, I prayed first. So often the children who live the farthest from the parent or parents are the ones judging the sibling who lives closest and is providing the countless hours of care each week. The sibling who is providing the support to the parent really needs their siblings trust, support, and above all prayers.

CHAPTER 4
Storms of My Own Making

The flight to Romania was quite long with a connection in Amsterdam. We landed at the airport in Bucharest and still had a few hours bus ride to the town of Fagaras. As we were waiting at the airport, the leader of our team, Dr. Prince, approached me and said, "I hear you were in full-time ministry." I had not shared that information on my application for the mission team. Dr. Prince then looked at me and announced, "Well, the pastor is expecting you to bring the word tomorrow morning!"

Wow, another God moment! I was very jet-lagged when we finally got to Camp Bit of Heaven. I went to bed and got up at like 4:00 a.m. Romania time and God laid a message on my heart to share with the people of the Romanian Church. My translator was a young man named Flavius. I never realized how our lives would intertwine in the days and years ahead.

In my message to the Romanian church, I told them about a boy who grew up out in the country. Most of his relatives and neighbors were either farmers or factory workers. Neither of his parents had gone to college. His church had a little school for about a hundred pupils that he attended. He came home from school one day when he was seven or eight years old and announced to his mom that when he grew up, he wanted to be a medical missionary!

His mom did not in any way tell him it was impossible. She just listened and nodded her head! Well, twenty years later this boy that grew up working on farms, graduated from dental school, and he was a "doctor" at age twenty-six. About ten years after that he graduated from seminary, and he was a "pastor" and a "doctor" but he was not a "medical missionary."

Fortyfive years after making this announcement to his mom, he finds himself in Romania on a mission team as a dentist, standing before you sharing the gospel. I am indeed a "medical missionary." I told the people in that church that if God could take a country boy like me from Michigan in the United States all the way to Romania to be a medical missionary, think of what he could do in each of their lives. With God nothing is impossible.

Monday through Friday our mission team set up in different small villages. Every person who came through met with our evangelists and heard the gospel and received a Romanian New Testament Bible before they could avail themselves to all our services. We provided a physician, three dentists, a pharmacy, eyeglasses, and had people ministering to the children.

This mission trip was life changing for me. The people we served in the little villages did not lead busy lives like us Americans. Their lives were very simple, but many of them seemed to have a peace I was looking for. The word that best described the mission trip's impact on me was perspective! My life was put into perspective.

I needed to slow down. My life needed to be downsized so I could more fully use my gifts to serve the Lord! I told the Lord I was returning in 2014 and every year I was able for the rest of my life. I was so blessed by serving in Romania and it was my sincere hope to share this experience with my dear wife Beth in 2014.

When our children were in high school, they asked to go on foreign mission trips and my answer was, "Why can't you do missions here in the United States?" I did not have a clue of the impact a mission trip could have on someone and their walk of faith.

I told my family that I would pay half the cost for anyone who wanted to serve the Lord on a mission trip. I planted the seed with my two oldest grandchildren who were five at the time. I told Calvin and Lexi that in nine years when they were fourteen, they could go on the mission trip to Romania. At the time of the writing of this book, they are both thirteen and looking forward to next year.

I kept reflecting on the trip in the weeks after arriving home. Pastor Jon and his wife Ani were the ones who worked with our American mission team leader to organize our trip and select the locations we would serve.

One night in Romania John shared a little bit about himself. He and Ani were both going to college to be veterinarians. The year before they were to graduate, they both gave their lives to the Lord. Neither one of them ever practiced veterinary medicine. They have been in full-time ministry the last twenty-five years.

Cristi and Daniella owned Camp Bit of Heaven where our mission team spent the week. When Christi was young his dad would whisper in his ear every night, "Our God is bigger than this communist regime, in my lifetime or in yours, God will take it down!"

Daniella's family finally caved to the pressure and quit gathering privately in groups to worship during the communist years. Daniella, at eight years old, wouldn't quit talking about Jesus so she was sent to a school to be brainwashed. After three weeks the headmaster said it wasn't working. Danielle wouldn't quit talking about "her Jesus!" Danielle finally said, "I'm not going back, what can they do?"

When I arrived back home, I started prayer walking the abandoned Girl Scout camp, Camp Kitchikippi, which was directly across the road from our house. The camp was on twenty acres overlooking a lake. The building was in great need of major renovation. But if it was God's plan he would provide.

I approached the owners about possibly purchasing the camp to use for youth and family ministries and for schools. I felt it would be a great way to honor their parents who had built the camp sixty years before. Our inquiry was not considered. Instead, the camp sold at an auction the next June.

Communism ended in Romania in 1989 when Cristi and Daniella were about twenty years old. At the time, Daniella told Cristi, "We can't waste this freedom!" Those words will stick with me for the rest of my life. Due to my own busyness, I was wasting the freedoms to share the gospel. As I came to this realization, it became evident to me that the main purpose for God allowing me to go on the mission trip was not so I could serve the Romanians. No, it was to serve as a wake-up call to me, Rod Knoerr!

God knew I had spent my life working hard, always busy, running around like a chicken with my head chopped off, trying to help people. I vowed to the Lord that I would change! Back from Romania, I would only be working three days a week as a dentist and no longer making that long commute. Perfect time to start *letting go* and *letting God*!

In October 2013, a couple of months after getting back from Romania, Beth and I purchased a run-down house four houses down from our house on the lake. We referred to this house as the "project house." My pie-in-the-sky dream was for this to be a bonding experience for my youngest son and me.

Our son Christian was recently engaged to be married to his high school sweetheart. He was living at home with Beth and me, attending a local college. I hoped to teach him a lot about home remodeling and maybe this could be a house he could buy when he got married in two years. We ended the transition year of 2013 at the beginning stages of the "project house."

As we started 2014, we were excited to start a year with no long commute to Flushing. We hoped to begin to settle into a calmer more balanced lifestyle, or so we thought. Beth and I didn't know it at the time, but the year 2014 would prove to be the beginning of a molding and shaping process for us as individuals and as a married couple.

I asked Beth if she would join me on the next mission trip in July. She was concerned what would happen if the plane went down. Our children and grandchildren would lose both their parents and grandparents. The trip had been so meaningful to me, and I wanted to share the experience with my honey.

Understand, neither of us were world travelers. I think this trip was a little out of Beth's comfort zone. I asked her to pray about it. About two weeks later she said, "I'm going to Romania." I was confused. She said she was in church singing, and she realized if Jesus could die on the cross for her, she could go to Romania.

In January, with the depressed housing market, it made sense to think it would be a good idea to buy a Victorian house built in the 1800s that had been converted into four one-bedroom apartments. We felt this could eventually be income property and it would give me something to do now that I did not own a dental practice. All four apartments had tenants. Our plan was to majorly renovate all four apartments. We were going to wait to renovate until each apartment was vacated.

I recalled the quote by Robert Burns, "The best laid plans of mice and men often go awry." Shortly after purchasing the Victorian house things began to change. The "project house" should have been called the "problem house." I had a structural engineer look at the foundation of the project house. The foundation was made of timbers, no concrete or cement blocks.

A very extensive renovation that would require jacking the house up and pouring footings and a new concrete foundation was just the beginning. I hired a foundation contractor, and we just didn't seem to see eye to eye. With about 75 percent of the foundation completed, we parted ways.

At the same time, the Victorian house that we purchased in January had tenants that we inherited. One of the first-floor tenants would regularly over drink alcohol and play his music very loud. The apartment above him had a married couple with a newborn baby. I kept getting phone calls in the middle of the night. I would talk to the first-floor tenant to no avail.

Long story short, after three months of problems— by the way he didn't pay his rent—the power company turned off his heat and he finally moved out. Soon after he moved out, the young couple also moved out. I now had two empty apartments to renovate and advertise for new tenants. Welcome to the world of being a landlord.

Oh, there is more! In Michigan we tend to do jobs in the winter inside our houses so that when warm weather comes, we can enjoy the outdoors. In February I decided to completely renovate and expand our upstairs bathroom. As I was removing the drywall on the outside wall, I discovered that we had issues with our roof leaking. Winter in Michigan made it difficult to replace the roof of our house. My plan was to wait until May to hire a roof contractor. Thus, we would have a bathroom stripped to the studs on one wall and on half of the ceiling for four months.

Since selling my dental practice almost a year previous, the simpler, stress-free life was not becoming a reality. Actually, I began to realize that there were storms of life that just come upon us and there were also *storms of our own making*. Too often we overestimate what we can do and underestimate the time required to complete a commitment. Guilty on both counts!

At the end of February our church was starting a new growth opportunity for men called "Fight Club." The name was based on a Bible verse from Nehemiah 4:14 where it says we are to spiritually fight for our wives our children and our homes. Fight Club was twelve weeks long. Daily and weekly assignments were made in four areas: spiritual, intellectual, relational, and physical. You received a strike if you didn't do an assignment. Three strikes and you were out. Men were placed in squads, and each man had an accountability partner. Each squad had a squad leader. I was one of the squad leaders.

This chapter of Fight Club was difficult and eye-opening for me. Some weeks I would do fifty push-ups and sit-ups four days of the week and run five miles. Our intellectual assignment each week was to read a chapter in a book that related to men. Spiritual assignments entailed reading chapters from the Bible, journaling, praying, and memorizing verses each week. We received relational assignments that involved our wives and children.

My goal for this Fight Club chapter was to discover how to experience "peace in the storm." It was during these twelve weeks that I began to develop some spiritual disciplines that I will continue for the rest of my life. Each morning I got up at 5:00 a.m. and read from the Bible, reflected, journaled, and prayed.

I always believed there was a benefit to reading the Bible and to prayer, but in the busyness of life I would often rush through my time with the Lord. I never spent enough quiet time with the Lord to allow my mind to slow down enough to really commune and hear from the Lord. Often if I tried to spend time with the Lord at night, I would fall asleep.

After reading a book where the author asked, "When do you tune an instrument, before or after the concert?" It was then that I realized I needed to spend time in the Bible and prayer prior to walking into the storms of life. It was amazing how differently I reacted to the difficult times of life. The great sixteenth-century reformer Martin Luther has been quoted as saying, "I have so much to do that I will spend the first three hours in prayer." That statement does not make earthly sense, but I was beginning to bear the fruit of starting my day with committed, quiet, reflective time with the Lord.

Fight Club was the beginning of the new me. I have always been two things, a hard worker and most definitely not a quitter! There was no way that I was going to get a strike in Fight Club. As a result, I was committed to complete every daily and weekly assignment. As I look back, I realize why Fight Club is twelve weeks long. I read somewhere that it takes about two months for a new habit to become automatic. Some of the assignments of Fight Club were becoming habits that would prove vital to me as I experienced the real storms of life that were coming.

As the chapter went on, I realized that in order to have a "peace in the storm," I needed to quit working harder but rather I need to "let go and let God." As I more and more surrendered, I more and more began to see glimpses of peace in my life. I had lived most of my life like a car with its rpms in the red zone. Life is not meant to be lived in the red zone continuously. When you live that way, you tend to be short on patience and exhibit a short fuse. My wife would tolerate the occasional blowups because she knew that whatever I was doing was usually for her and my dear children. I was a talented, hardworking guy; but my name was Rod not God!

As I spent regular quality time with the Lord, I more and more realized the storm I was experiencing was my fault. *I* decided to buy the "project house." *I* decided to buy the rental property. *I* decided to tear apart the upstairs bathroom. If I tried to pour myself into all three of these projects, the storm would only intensify.

Fight Club was definitely helping me see that my choices, I emphasize *my* choices, had spread me quite thin. As I went through the Fight Club graduation in May, I vowed to continue to downsize and be more realistic on the busyness in my life. Short temper and lack of patience was definitely improving as I quit trying to be "Super Rod!"

With Beth's help, I did renovate the two apartments during the spring. By June we had two new tenants! I hired a roofer to reroof our house and I fought my normal self and decided I would be in no hurry to remodel the bathroom. I also decided I would not worry about the project house until Beth and I returned from Romania in August. A book has margins, the words don't fill the entire page. My life needed margins for rest, reflection, refilling through God's word, and for time to handle unplanned circumstances.

Over the last year since I sold the dental practice, I was available to babysit Lexi, soon to be five, and Liam, soon to be one, on my day off while my daughter Kari and Beth worked as a dental hygienists. I started doing this when Liam was six weeks old. Beth had been watching Lexi one or two days a week since our sweetheart was less than a year old. We were so blessed by our little honey babies.

The slower pace allowed Beth and me to really focus more on

the blessings of our family. Four married children and our youngest was engaged to be married. Six beautiful grandchildren that loved coming to our lake house and were like "little fish" in the water. As we enjoyed the beauty of the lake God had provided, we weren't aware of the "storm clouds of life" that were gathering in the distance!

REFUGE REFLECTIONS

1. If you were going into battle, would you wait till after the battle to put on your armor?

   How ridiculous, right! In the book of Ephesians it talks about putting on a spiritual armor, so we are prepared for the spiritual battles we face. Fight Club changed my life! I will forever start every morning with a time in God's word, reflection, prayer, and journaling. Putting on my spiritual armor every morning has changed my life and how I deal with the storms of life each day. I encourage you to start each day putting on your spiritual armor. How can you start?

2. Can you relate to *storms of my own making*? So often in life we look to blame our circumstances or someone else for the stress or the situation where we find ourselves. I am asking you to step back and look at your life. Can you see where you may be the one who made the choices resulting in the storm you are currently in?

3. Are you in a place where you need to learn how to live the phrase, "less is more?" Sometimes the choices we have made individually are not bad things. Yet, as I said, we are not God. We only have so much time or energy. Where do you need to start?

CHAPTER 5

The Perfect Storm

Fight Club had impressed on me the need to surrender, to let go and let God. I needed to do less, say less, and let God take the lead in my life. The project house was one thing I decided to not put energy into. From February until the end of June I did not work at the project house, so that my life would be more balanced.

I wanted to finish stabilizing the foundation with a new contractor so I could begin the extensive renovation. I sure wanted to find a contractor with integrity. I prayed for a man who did what he said. We were leaving on the mission trip in a month. I hoped to get some good advice so I could get back to the project house when we returned from Romania.

In February I slid into the ditch on an icy road on the way to work. A man by the name of John stopped and pulled me out. He gave me his business card. He was the building inspector for a neighboring town and he was also a heating and cooling contractor. I paid John to come out and give me some advice. God works in amazing ways! It was no coincidence that John pulled me out of the ditch and I kept his card for four months.

Based on John's advice, I decided to do a large amount of demolition prior to having a contractor finish the foundation. I purchased this project house with the hope of this being a bonding experience with my youngest son who was in college and working. Christian was very busy with college and working two jobs.

My dear wife Beth and I ended up spending a lot of time in June and July demolishing concrete slabs and stabilizing the house. Because I had downsized a lot of the busyness in my life, Beth and I were able to complete all the demolition by ourselves with minimal help from our son. It was a real blessing spending time with Beth on the project house!

In July, prior to leaving for Romania, the dermatologist couldn't seem to help Beth with the constant itchiness associated with her eczema. Beth had dealt with the consequences of eczema her entire life. She would use various topical creams to treat the outbreaks. When she had a severe flair up, her dermatologist would prescribe a topical steroid cream.

They would always let her know that it wasn't good for her to use these steroid creams on a regular basis. Yet, the last few years it seemed like even regular use of topical steroids was not working. We got rid of family pets, tried special diets, removed carpet from our house, anything that could possibly help her eczema.

After really no help from the dermatologist, we did what all twenty-first century people do, we began to do research on the internet. We quickly found a large community of individuals who were dealing with the same issue. It appeared that the only answer was to quit using topical steroid creams. It was then that we became aware of the abbreviation TSW (topical steroid withdrawal). We discovered that people who were able to discontinue topical steroids eventually quit experiencing dermatological eczema flare-ups. There was one big problem, the *withdrawal process*!

There was no significant difference between weaning off the topical steroids or going off them "cold turkey." The disadvantage of going off the steroids slowly was that the withdrawal process would take longer. The withdrawal described on the internet would entail many nights of insomnia, shivers, skin that feels like bugs are crawling all over you. The urge to itch is so intense that a person would itch themselves to the point of bleeding. For days areas of skin are all scabby. Yet, a week later, liquid is weeping from the skin. On top of this, there was always a great chance of infection.

Why would anyone choose to go through this withdrawal nightmare? Because of story after story of people who were now symptom free for the first time in their lives. Our twenty-eight-year-old daughter Kristi at the time, also had eczema and was suffering with the steroids not working, while being the mother of three young children ages six, four, and one. The problem with withdrawal is it generally took at least two years before the awful withdrawal side effects ended.

After much research and prayer, much discussion with Beth, Kristi, her husband Jon, and me, we decided to go off the topical steroids after we got back from Romania in August. Our attitude was that this storm of TSW was a defined length of time. It would be worth it. We would rely on God and each other!

In July, I returned to Romania as a member of a medical/dental mission team. My dear wife Beth joined the team this year for the first time. We were so blessed to be a blessing to others. We both worked in the dental clinic together. God again emphasized that sometimes less is more. Life was so busy here in the US. We both came home looking forward to quickly finishing the project house. We both were wholeheartedly committed to moving toward a more peaceful, less busy life!

The Saturday after we arrived back from Romania, Beth and I hosted what was now the fifth annual Knoerr pig roast. This yearly gathering continued to be a time for us to thank the Lord for all our blessings. We invited neighbors, relatives, church friends, and coworkers. My wife's amazing gift of hospitality was on full display for all to see. Beth in her totally grace-filled, stress-free manner hosted anywhere from 75–150 people each year. This year was another great gathering!

As we moved into September, both Beth and Kristi began to experience increased TSW side effects. Major itchiness, insomnia, tiredness due to lack of sleep. I did see a sign from God that he was breaking me, causing me to surrender, so I could be the husband, father, man of God that God himself intended.

During a church service—I will never forget the date, September 28, 2014—I looked down at my crossed legs and witnessed something I had never seen in my life. My foot was not moving! My entire life I always had a nervous energy. I always had a foot moving when it was crossed. My foot was totally still! I whispered to my wife Beth, "Look at my foot!"

She had been married to me for thirty-five years; she whispered, "It's not moving." God was breaking me and starting to give me a peace that only he could give. I was starting to experience, "peace in the storm." Little did I know that I didn't have a clue what a *real* storm was like. But God knew one was coming!

After completing and acting as a squad leader in our church's first chapter of Fight Club in the spring, I decided to participate in another Fight Club. I knew that I needed the structure and the community of other men. Having an accountability partner that I met with every week was something I had never experienced in my life. With the project house and now Beth and Kristi's TSW, I needed a community of men around me to point me to the Lord and keep me accountable! At the same time Beth was a part of a Wednesday morning women's Bible study that brought her great comfort and support!

John, the building inspector who pulled me out of the ditch, gave me some great advice, and based on his recommendations I hired a new foundation contractor who did a great job and finished the foundation by September. I also hired a contractor who was willing to work with me and my son. Jim turned out to be a gift from God. Things seemed to be turning around. By November, the house was enclosed, roof was on, and vinyl siding was being installed.

Even though I was trying to simplify my life and slow down, I was still operating pretty near empty. I was operating on the assumption that if I worked really hard, life would slow down once the house was done. Boy, was I wrong! There were so many things I had to do at the project house after work and on weekends. I now was becoming aware of the fact I was not "Super Rod." Fight Club's emphasis on time with the Lord and leaning on your brothers was the difference between losing it and barely surviving. I was part of another group of men who graduated from our second chapter of Fight Club in November.

The last half of 2014 was the first six months of my life where I got up at 5:00 a.m. every morning and spent at least an hour in prayer, reading the Bible, reflecting, and journaling. As a result, I was much more patient and understanding that my youngest son was almost never available to help me on the project house. Remember, I bought the house "assuming" it would be a great bonding time with him.

Because I wasn't operating entirely in the red zone, I was becoming much more patient. I actually did not fly off the handle when the contractor put the wrong siding on the front of the house and when subcontractors over and over did not show up when they said they would and when deadline after deadline was not met.

The more I tried to surrender to God in the storm, the more the intensity of the storm seemed to increase. I am sure many people have experienced this and have gotten mad at God or went back to their old way of living. As I look back in my journals, I realized that God knew I needed to really be beat down so I would truly surrender and let go and let God.

Hebrews 12:5–7 says, "My son, do not make light of the Lord's discipline, and do not lose heart when he rebukes you, because the Lord disciplines the ones He loves, and he chastens everyone he accepts as his son. Endure hardship as discipline, God is treating you as His children. For what children are not disciplined by their father." God loved me enough to truly rain down on me with storm after storm to make sure my surrender would be true and lasting.

As we ended 2014, the contractors were getting close to being done. Then it would be up to me to paint the entire interior of the house and to install cabinets, install all the doors, do all the finish woodwork, and install an entire house of laminate flooring. What was I thinking? But at the time I thought I could see the end in sight. Here comes 2015.

When we returned from Romania, I planned to be realistic on the time frame for the completion of the project house. Little did I know that there would be delay after delay after delay. The drywall could not be completed until there was working heat. The heat could not be made operational until there was a chimney. The mason who said the chimney would be done in October would prove to finish it in February 2015. But I was much more patient than a year ago with the first foundation contractor. I actually was praying for the contractors, and I was leaving the worrying to the Lord, "Only do what only you can do."

I began journaling each morning during my quiet time in 2014. I started 2015 with reflections of 2014 and goals for 2015. When I started Fight Club in February of last year my goal was to have "peace in the storm." As 2014 progressed it became very apparent to me that the storm I was living in was of my own making. So, I was starting 2015 with much more realistic expectations of how much I could accomplish while staying out of the red zone and more and more being at peace and not stressed out.

Beth and my daughter Kristi were almost five months into TSW as we began 2015. Beth was constantly in discomfort. Itchiness, insomnia, chills, and being very tired was life. Dry scaly skin for a few days, followed by wet oozing skin for periods of time. Many times, this affected her and Kristi's face. My son-in-law Jon and I really were stepping to the plate to be as supportive and helpful as possible. This TSW withdrawal was much more difficult than we could have imagined. But Beth and I had been doing this partnership in life for over thirty-five years. This was supposed to be a defined period of two years. Together we would survive this storm.

On top of all the physical challenges of TSW, my eighty-seven-year-old father-in-law fell in December and had to have surgery to remove bleeding on his brain. He lived about two hours away from us, living independently. He returned home from the hospital with a catheter. Beth went to visit him and discovered that he was unaware that his bag had come unhooked from his catheter and he had been leaking all over his carpet for days.

My dear father-in-law Harold was the most godly, gentle, servant-minded person I ever met. He never gave me advice on how to be a husband or father. He just led by example. He was amazing, but he was mentally slipping, and it was time for him to no longer be independent, especially two hours away from us. After much prayer we realized he either had to go to an adult care facility or move in with us. We decided to have him move in with us. At the beginning of February, we placed a hospital bed in our living room because he could not safely navigate our steps to the second floor where all our bedrooms were located.

In January our third granddaughter and seventh grandchild Kallie was born at Oaklawn Hospital in Marshall. It had been well over a year since my oldest son Rod had cut off all communication with us. Rod was not only named after me, he had the same strong will as I had. We seemed to lock horns most of his life. I loved him with all my heart and because of that at times I would offer my opinion and, needless to say, it only made matters worse and I drove us apart!

As God was breaking me in 2015, I began to realize that often as parents we need to pray more and trust God. For over a year my prayer had been for God to use a person or situation to bring Rod and Danielle closer to God and to us. Every month or so I would text him a short caring text. When we heard Danielle was going to deliver their baby we decided to quietly drop off a gift at the nurses station. We had not seen our grandson Kaden since he was one; he was now about two and a half years old. Our job was to pray and rely on God!

It was the end of February before the project house was ready for me to start painting and installing floors and doing all the wood trim work. Beth was doing awful with the TSW and at the time we moved her dad Harold in with us. We were also beginning to try to help Kristi as she was also dealing with TSW while mothering a six, four, and two-year-old.

It was during the lull in the project house that I realized that I was the real "project." A year ago, I was angry with a foundation contractor and let him know it. God was starting to get my attention. I needed to *trust* him. So often in my life I would open my mouth feeling like I was helping. Look what it had done to my relationship with my dear son. God was teaching me to pray more, say less, and trust him to take care of things!

A year after the first Fight Club, I found myself praying for the contractors instead of voicing frustration. I had paid a plumber half up-front and the rest would be at completion. I left voicemails and texts for weeks with no response. I needed him to plumb a drain so the furnace installer could move forward. I ended up hiring another plumber to install this drain.

I finally texted the plumber and asked him if anything was wrong because I would pray for him. He almost immediately called me. He was having marital issues and he was having to put his mom in a nursing home. Often when we are experiencing storms in our own life, we want to blame others for our storm instead of acknowledging that we are really in the storms together and we both need to look to the only one who is with us in the storm and can calm the storm, Jesus!

During this time, where Beth was really struggling with tiredness and extreme itching, I was so blessed by her godly caring heart. Realize, my wife is a gentle, behind the scenes, under the radar servant. Beth was working two days a week as a dental hygienist, and she came home from work and shared with me what she had done in the staff meeting. Beth told her fellow staff members that at Judgement Day she didn't want to be the neighbor/friend who didn't tell her coworkers about Jesus. What boldness of faith. Wow!

Because of the delays with contractors, I was not able to work on the project house in February. God knew the plan all along. Beth's dad would move into our house in February and Beth's TSW sleepless nights, fatigue, and itchiness would be worse. I had more time to help Beth with her dad and to help her in any way I could.

I decided that I needed more than ever the accountability and support of another chapter of Fight Club. So, at the beginning of March, I started my third chapter of Fight Club as a squad leader. One of our relational assignments in Fight Club was to pray with your spouse. Both Beth and I are people of prayer, and we have off and on prayed together over the years but not on a regular basis.

In March I began to spend 20–30 hours a week painting and working on the project house. During that time, I was also working in two dental offices. One week I worked over thirty hours on the project house. I thought if I worked long and hard enough, I would eventually have balance. Yet, I was feeling so guilty going over to work on the project house while leaving Beth with her dad.

Because of the Fight Club assignment, I asked Beth to pray with me. Because I am the vocal one, I asked her to start the prayer. She began by saying, "Please God, forgive me that I have not been able to go over to the house and help Rod more!" What a powerful lesson for our marriage! We were both feeling guilty for not helping the other one more. Yet when we prayed together, we became aware of the concerns and caring of the other one. This was a huge affirmation of the great value of praying together as a couple. From that time on we made prayer together a regular priority.

As we moved into April, I began to realize that all the time over the years I worked on remodeling houses I was focused more on my needs or wants and not God's desires. When I was weary or stressed that definitely impacted my Christian witness to others. So my intent in April as we were moving Beth's Dad into his own apartment that was located less than a half mile from our house was to try to work less on the project house.

The plan was for Beth to lay out Dad's medications every day and help him grocery shop. We knew he was starting to slip mentally, and he really may only have another year to live somewhat independently. With Dad moving down the street I must have subconsciously felt Beth would be less busy with her dad, which was not the case. So, I reverted back to my old self and started working way too many hours on the house in hopes of finally completing the project house.

Within a day or two after dad moved out, I had a stressful day at work. I had some frustrating conversations with the contractors and on top of that, spent some long evenings at the project house. My tank was empty and I was running on fumes. I came home from working on the project house and I shared with Beth all the stress I was feeling and I just lost it. I will call it "the great chandelier awakening." I had gotten a beer out of the refrigerator and had only taken a sip when it happened. I threw the almost full bottle of beer at the chandelier over our dining room table. It was a direct hit! I will never forget that "coosh" sound.

My sweet dear wife did not say a word. She quietly went upstairs to our bedroom. I quickly realized I had really made a mess and guess who had something to clean up. I cleaned up all the spilled beer and broken pieces of facets from the chandelier. I sat down and contemplated before going upstairs to my wife. I apologized to her and told her I would forever be changed. I finally realized God had been throwing storm after storm after storm in hopes of breaking me! So often I was close to surrendering and then would return to my old ways. This "chandelier awakening" broke me. Things would be different! I would be different!

I would never work at the pace of "Super Rod" anymore. I decided to either put less time into the project house, ask for more help from my son, or hire people to do some of the work. I was so embarrassed and yet at the same time so thankful that God was humbling and teaching me. By the way, we had extra facets to fix the chandelier. Thank you, Jesus, for loving me enough to break me so you could help me find "peace in the storm."

The next night I got a phone call at 11 p.m. I figured it was my sister calling me about our dad. It was my younger brother's wife.

I will never forget her words, "*Todd is gone!*" My brother had been driving his all-terrain 4-wheeler with a friend. He did not have his seat belt on and flipped the vehicle. Instantly he had broken his neck and was gone. My brother was only fifty-four years old. Another opportunity for life learning. Slow down and enjoy the moments. Life is short. Todd's passing just really emphasized what the Lord was teaching me.

In May I had a great conversation with my youngest son Christian and his fiancée Emily. They were getting married in August. Beth and I asked them if they would be interested in buying the project house. We would sell the house to them with no money down on a two-year land contract. This would allow them to get established after college in their careers and then they could pay us off with a conventional home loan.

They definitely wanted the house. Christian committed to help on the house. Christian really worked hard in May and early June. I hired someone to do the wood trim around all the windows on the interior of the house. Can you believe I hired someone instead of doing it myself? I finally started to realize, to honor God, I needed help! The project house, with my son's help, was coming along, the real project, me was finally surrendering!

The graduation ceremony for my third Fight Club chapter was toward the end of May. Fight Club, with its assignments and accountability partners had been instrumental in the process of breaking me. I was truly beginning to experience the "peace in the storm" that was my goal for the first chapter over a year ago. In fact, I was awarded the "Spirit of Fight Club" award as voted on by my Fight Club brothers. This award is given to the Fight Club brother that has done the most to support and encourage his fellow brothers and who most exemplifies the Fight Club Creed. I was so humbled to receive the award.

Even though Beth's TSW symptoms were awful, after much prayer it was evident God wanted us to be a part of the medical/dental mission team to Romania. This would be my third trip and

Beth's second trip. We would be going in June, not July, this year. We had an unbelievable week serving the Lord in Romania. Over 1,000 people were seen by our team. Beth served in the triage area. She was the face of our team, meeting people, taking health histories, and coordinating what each person needed in terms of our ministries. Beth's translator was the Romanian pastor's wife, Daniella. They were an amazing team. As weary as my dear honey was, the love of Jesus shined out from her beautiful green eyes. Beth's kind, gentle spirit allowed her to really connect with many of our translators. She was so encouraging to so many people in spite of her awful TSW symptoms.

For the first time in my life, I spent Father's Day without seeing any of our children. I did get to talk with them on Facebook. I really missed them, but I felt our example of service to others was what I hoped they were seeing as Beth and I were on the other side of the world. My oldest son's birthday was while we were in Romania. This would make two years that we had not seen our dear son or talked to him on his birthday. We continued to pray, trusting that God had a plan and someday God would bring us back together.

Just a couple weeks after coming back from Romania, I helped Beth host our sixth annual pig roast. She is such an amazing hostess. This was our yearly gift to our friends, neighbors, and relatives. Most people would be stressed leading up to hosting 100–150 people. Not my sweetheart.

Beth was born to be a hostess. She was just like her mom. God truly gave her the gift of hospitality. Even with her awful TSW, she never once expressed stress or a desire to not have the pig roast. When Beth was focused on hosting others, doing what she was created by God to do, she just didn't dwell on the storm of TSW.

I think so many people use the storms of life as an excuse to focus on their sufferings instead of using the gifts God has given them to bless others while they are in the midst of life's storms. We were learning that the more we waited on the Lord each day and grew closer as a couple, God would really do some great things as we focused on his path while we were in the midst of the storm!

July quickly flew by. We finished the project house the week before Christian and Emily's wedding. It was ready for them to move into after their wedding.

REFUGE REFLECTIONS

1. Are you now or have you ever experienced a time in your life that the harder you tried to find balance in your life, the more ridiculous it got?

2. Are you waiting on the Lord for discernment and for strength as you try to make changes in your life?

3. Who can you go to for support and to seek counsel?

4. Even though you are making changes and your life still seems way too busy and out of control doesn't mean that you aren't on the right track. If you are moving in a direction that will allow you to be more fully used by the Lord, he will walk with you and guide and encourage you like he did for me as I was trying to complete the project house!"

CHAPTER 6
The Winds of Change

Beth and I were blessed with the birth of our third grandchild of the year, Landry (grandchild number 9), one week before the wedding. Big sister Kari wouldn't be missing her little brother's wedding. The wedding day was awesome. To see Christian and Emily united in marriage before the Lord! All five of our children were now married to fellow Christians. Our grandchildren were all in homes where they would know the Lord and be nurtured in the faith.

In spite of how tired Beth must have felt, she was just beaming with joy and pride. I will never forget watching Beth dancing the "Mother/Son" dance. Watching my beautiful sweetheart with her baby boy was the high point of the night for me. Beth's Dad at eighty-eight was able to attend. At the time, we didn't really know how special it was to have Dad at the wedding.

We had survived the storms of the rental house problems, the project house. We were now entering a new stage of our marriage after thirty-six years. God was slowly breaking me to surrender! We were going home after Christian and Emily's wedding to an empty house, no children or parents, for the first time in thirty-six years! At the time we didn't use the phrase, "empty nest." We had no inkling what God had in store!

Just days after the wedding, I am in the dental office and I get a call from my oldest son's wife. It had been over eighteen months

55

since we had seen them. Their baby Kallie was seven months old and our grandson Kaden had just turned three. I had been daily praying, "God, please use a person or an event to bring Rod closer to you Lord and to us." My love for Rod that often led me to give him advice or correction had pushed him away! God had slowly been breaking me to realize my job was to pray.

Rod had a heavenly Father who loved him. I was learning if I was patient and prayed more that God would often take care of things. The contribution God needed from me was often quite minimal and subtle. I prayed to be open to when God wanted to use me. Then my daughter-in-law Danielle informed us Rod had a sudden change in his employment situation and she was concerned! She actually asked if we would be open to talk with her and help. She didn't know how much we had prayed and how much we loved them.

I was leaping for joy inside. This could be the opportunity that I had been praying for. My prayer was now that I could be God's instrument and that I could "let go and let God" and above all not open my big mouth. I had been praying for this opportunity. He ended up losing his management job. A week later we were invited to their house. I will never forget our seven-month-old granddaughter Kallie who we saw for the first time. Her arms were extended to us, like we had been part of her life the last seven months.

I was again praying about being a squad leader for our church's fourth chapter of Fight Club that would start in the middle of September. The leaders and I had been praying for Rod for over a year. We had a Fight Club leader's meeting a few days after Danielle's phone call. I told my Fight Club brothers that I felt God was wanting me to possibly invite Rod to participate in this next chapter of Fight Club.

My brothers in Christ thought I was out of my mind! I hadn't seen him in almost two years, I was just renewing a relationship with him. They all felt I would be seen as pushy and it could really backfire on me. The more I prayed the more I felt Rod was supposed to be a part of our new Fight Club chapter.

At the same time Beth and Kristi were completing the first year of TSW and it was awful. Just unbelievable itchiness and insomnia. Obviously, when you don't sleep well, you are always weary! Beth was just truly amazing. She always focused on serving others. With five married children and now nine grandchildren, Beth was always preparing meals and hosting. She was in her element shopping for birthday presents and Christmas gifts for our family that now numbered twenty-one! Beth started Christmas shopping in August. Always looking for a deal. God truly was giving this woman the energy to be wife, mom, grandma as we entered September.

Well, the next time I saw Rod I told him how Fight Club was changing me. My short fuse was disappearing and I was much more patient. I told him I would have to prove to him over time that I was really changed. I didn't invite him to be a part of Fight Club. I didn't tell him how Fight Club would be good for him. I just shared how God was breaking a stubborn guy like me and what a difference it was making in my life.

Over the next few days that feeling I was to invite Rod wouldn't go away. The next time I saw him, I told him "I know you are in a major transition with a lot of uncertainty, but I wanted you to know you are welcome to be a part of this fall's chapter of Fight Club."

Our church decided to start a shorter and more moderate version of Fight Club for women called Journey. Beth was asked to be one of the leaders. As bad as her TSW was after prayer she decided it would be good to focus on serving others in the midst of her TSW storm. I was so proud of her! Beth was usually the quiet, under the radar, servant person. She didn't usually step out front. In spite of the awful TSW, she was saying, "Here I am Lord, use me!"

My fifty-seventh birthday was on a Thursday, Sept 10, a day that I would never forget. My father-law Harold had been living in a small apartment a half mile from our house for the last five months. Beth would take him his pills for the day every morning. He was becoming a little senile and we didn't trust him to lay out his daily pills. I got a call from Beth right after arriving at work. She had gone to her father's apartment, and she found him lying face down next to his bed. He had passed away in the night. I rushed from the office to be with my dear wife.

Dad had put on a Christian T-shirt I had given him twenty years earlier. I had never seen him wear it. On the front it said, "Loyal to the One, God's only Son." There was a Bible verse on the back, 1 John 4:9, "This is how God showed His love among us, He sent His one and only Son into the world that we might live through Him." Dad was an amazing man, even in his last moments he was pointing people to Jesus! Beth was sad but happy also. She knew her dad was mentally slipping. She really did not want Dad to end up in a care facility. God graciously took him home to heaven.

I loved that man so much. It truly was the *death of a legend*! He was such a gentle, giving, loving man. He never once told me how to be a good husband or father. He just led by example. My parents were married for fifty-five years, but I never saw the servant's heart in my dad that I saw in Beth's dad. My dad never washed dishes. Beth's dad always washed the dishes.

I learned so much from just watching dad. I figured if Beth lovingly took the time to daily prepare great meals, the least I could do was to clean up after and do the dishes. I was so blessed recently, as I watched my son-in-law Jon begin to wash dishes at our house recently. Dad had passed his servant attitude to at least two generations.

I led an intimate memorial service at the funeral home the night before Dad's funeral. Many people shared stories about this great man. In the book of Ephesians it says to, "love your wife as Christ loved the church and gave his life for it." Dad loved Beth's Mom like that. I remember when Dad retired, that was the last time Mom vacuumed the house. Dad loved his sweetheart so much, there was nothing he wouldn't do to show her his love. I actually told everyone at the memorial that dad "adored" and literally "cherished" Beth's Mom like one would cherish fine crystal. I wanted to more and more become that kind of a husband.

The Friday after dad's funeral we had our Fight Club midnight meeting. Anyone who was possibly interested could come and then they had to commit to the ten-week chapter by the following Monday. I had not mentioned anything to Rod for the last couple of weeks. That afternoon Rod said to me, "I'm going to the Fight Club meeting tonight!" The next day he told me he would sign up to do the ten-week chapter. Wow, there truly is power in prayer!

In late September, with everything going on in our lives, I showed Beth an advertisement for joining the John Maxwell Team. John has written more books on leadership than anyone in history. I had read many of his books over the years. John was spreading his influence by certifying leadership coaches, trainers, and speakers.

I had left dentistry for ten years and was involved in church ministry. I had always been drawn to helping others realize their God given potential. When I showed Beth the opportunity and investment involved, she said, "You have to do this!" I began to take many online courses looking forward to the Live Certification event in Orlando, Florida, in March 2016.

In spite of Beth's weariness from TSW, she completed the first women's Journey chapter. She was the oldest woman by far at fifty-eight to do Journey. Only with God's help could Beth have had the energy to do all the physical assignments! God knew young women needed to be exposed to Beth's gentle, organized, resilient spirit! Beth and I also decided to start hosting a small group in our home every Thursday evening. Without God's power and encouragement there is no way Beth could do what she was doing!

As we moved into October, I prayed about how to encourage Rod and Danielle. They were living about forty-five minutes from Beth and me. I kept getting this feeling that Rod, Danielle, Kallie, and Kaden should move in with us during their time of transition. It did not make earthly sense. We had not talked in over eighteen months until six weeks before and now I was feeling God wanted Beth and me to invite Rod and Danielle and the kids to move in with us.

I shared my thoughts with Beth and she was in total agreement! I had an idea that Beth and I could give them a loan to buy a fixer-upper house and Rod could renovate and flip the house as a way to support them. Rod was always handy with his hands and was always learning from me and eager to help when I renovated our houses.

During October I began to feel, due to Beth's TSW, she should quit her job. She was working two days a week as a dental hygienist in the same dental office that our daughter Kari worked. One week Beth's face would be all scabs, the next week it was wet and ulcerated. Beth didn't want to leave her dentist until Kari returned to work from maternity leave.

Rod and Danielle and kids did indeed move in with us at the end of October. Within a couple of weeks, Beth's TSW was getting so bad that her face was breaking out and weeping to the point she was getting infections and was being placed on antibiotics. I didn't feel it was safe for her to continue working as a dental hygienist. With all the open sores on her face, she was so susceptible to infections. I encouraged Beth to quit her job in November. Beth finally agreed with me. At the time we did not have a clue how bad the TSW experience would get, but God did!

Beth was again the organizer for the Thanksgiving dinner at our church for 350 people. She felt so self-conscious of her face. Her poor face really did look awful. Most people would have been embarrassed and would have asked someone else to serve as the organizer. I encouraged Beth that she was such a blessing to the members of our church and all the volunteers. Any one close to us knew what she was going through.

I gently encouraged her not to worry about what others thought! We approached TSW with the attitude, "keep on keeping on." I always looked forward to the afternoon before the dinner. After the second church service, members would set up all the tables and chairs. Then Beth and I would be left alone for the afternoon to organize and do all the tablecloths and table decorations Beth had chosen. I was so blessed to assist my wife in her area of giftedness. Her joy and glow outshined her facial ulcers and scabs.

At the end of November Rod began work on his first flip house. When I had time, I would help him. Beth was watching Kari and Zach's three kids two days a week and we also had little Kaden, age three, and Kallie, almost one, living with us. So often when people are going through what Beth was going through, they distance themselves from others. Beth was immersed in what brought her the greatest joy, her kids and grandkids! God knew the storm was going to increase so he was surrounding us with love and support.

Not only did Rod II and I complete the rigorous ten-week chapter of Fight Club, but so did my youngest, newly married son Christian, and my son-in-law Zach. To many, Fight Club looked like just another add on to ones already busy schedule. Fight Club on the other hand helped each of us with our priorities.

I can't emphasize enough how starting every day with at least an hour with the Lord changed the way I went through the day. Men are good at talking about sports. But when it came to real stuff like marriage and parenting concerns, men often try to do it on their own. I was finding a brotherhood I had never experienced, a brotherhood that I would so need to lean on in the days ahead. Rod and I were developing a friendship that I only could have dreamed of!

So many people are looking for a reason to play the victim. Beth had every reason to shut down and limp along. Not my sweet honey. She continued to seasonally decorate our house like no other. From summer, to Halloween, to Thanksgiving, to Christmas season. Our house was just magical. Beth lovingly shopped and wrapped literally hundreds of gifts for our ten married children and nine grandchildren. Each grandchild had the exact same number of gifts to open. It was the same with our children. Beth was in her element living out her primary love language, Acts of Service.

I was more and more learning how to serve my honey. I would do anything to bring relief or joy to her. I was discovering that my greatest joy was assisting Beth as she used her gifts to bring joy to others. The year 2015 was about truly experiencing the winds of change. My brother Todd and Beth's Dad were called to their eternal homes in Heaven! Three new healthy, beautiful grandbabies were born—Kallie, Lincoln, and Landry. Christian and Emily were married. Beth and I, with God's help were learning to experience, peace in the storm.

REFUGE REFLECTIONS

1. Do you have a mentor in your life, like my dear father-in-law? If you don't, spend time thinking and praying about possible people who you could approach to be your mentor.

2. The Fight Club men's ministry and the women's Journey ministry were vital places where Beth and I found relationships that we so needed. Do you have a place where you have people who are in similar life situations like you? If there are no such groups at your church look to other places for group love, support, and encouragement.

3. Are you estranged from someone in your life? Like with my son Rod, sometimes you are not the answer to restoring the relationship. Go to the Lord regularly in prayer. Periodically send short texts to the person so that they know you haven't forgot them and that you do indeed love them.

4. God may use someone or something else to start the restoration. I realized there was nothing I could do to restore my relationship with my son, so I prayed that the Lord would bring a person or a situation into Rod's life. I prayed that I would be ready and have the right words when that time came!

5. If you have given up on an estranged friend or loved one, remember it is never too late!

CHAPTER 7

What's Today, What's Tomorrow?

As we entered 2016, the Bible verse from James 1:2–4 came to mind, "Consider it pure joy my brothers whenever you face trials of many kinds. Because you know that the testing of your faith develops perseverance. Perseverance must finish its work so that you may be mature and complete, not lacking anything." God was using the various trials and afflictions to mold Beth and I so that God could do a great work through us!

I was asked to bring the message at our church in Marshall on the Sunday after New Year's. Everyone is thinking of New Year's resolutions at this time of year. What can I try to do different? What habit could I start; exercise, diet, reading the Bible? Over the last couple of years as God had been humbling me and breaking me, I came to realize that I needed to spend more time waiting on the Lord instead of charging forward in my own strength.

The title of my message was "Restolution for 2016." The whole theme of the message was that in order to know where we are going and what we are to be doing we need to spend time with the Lord— regular, daily, quality time with the Lord. This is not just a time where we do all the talking. I had a lot of experience going to God and talking. We needed to "rest" with the Lord.

We are commanded by God to bring our requests to him. But what good is that if we don't be quiet and listen for his response! My encouragement was to make a resolution to daily rest in the presence of the Lord. As we more and more rest with him, we will more and more find the peace, strength, and direction that only he could give.

Beth and Kristi were about eighteen months into the TSW. Many on the internet TSW support groups seemed to indicate the symptoms would start reducing at about twenty-four months. We were counting down the days in hopes this awful itchy, sleepless, painful experience was nearing its end. The first two weeks of January were just awful. Beth had committed to journal daily in 2016. My dear sweetheart was the most kind, gentle, grace-filled woman I had ever met.

Beth never spoke a cross word and most definitely never swore. Yet in her journal on January 4, sixteen months into TSW, my sweetheart actually used a swear word to describe her incessant pain! Trust me she had to have been at her limit to make a comment like that! Beth's skin was burning and painful sometimes and extremely dry and itchy other times. It seemed like she got one so-so night for every three bad nights. Warm apple vinegar baths were soothing, but it was like a double-edged sword. The bath would give her temporary relief from the itching but then dry out Beth's skin and make her even more itchy.

In the middle of the night, Beth started going downstairs on the couch so she wouldn't interrupt my sleep. I told Beth that we are in this together. I can't sleep when she isn't next to me and I can't help her if she needs me. I told her to ask me for help. The next night I found Beth again on our living room couch. I finally asked her this hard question, "You are afraid that with me going to work and staying up much of the night to help you, I will reach my limit and lose my cool and blow up?"

Beth didn't answer. When I think back to key moments in our marriage, what happened next was one of those milestone moments that would signal the beginning of a marital closeness that we never could have imagined. Beth was the epitome of a servant. She lived to care for her children and grandchildren. She was always available for others, including me. She was also not one to ask for help because she was the one always helping others.

Beth was the epitome of a humble servant to those around her. She was the most unbelievable daughter, wife, mother, grandmother, friend! She was born with the gift to graciously serve others. It was becoming more and more evident to me that as God was changing me, I needed to be for Beth what she had been for me the last almost forty years—a servant, cheerleader, encourager, sounding board.

Beth needed to know that I was unconditionally infatuated with her. It was time for me to truly live out our marriage vows, *to have and to hold from this day forth, for better or for worse, for richer, for poorer, in sickness and in health, to love and to cherish from this day forward until death do us part.*

Gary Chapman wrote the book, "The Five Love Languages." He says there are five ways we give and receive love. Beth's primary love language most definitely was *Acts of Service*. When Beth didn't answer me, I told her over the last year God had begun to break me. I was becoming a different man! I asked her to test me to see if I was a different man to see if I would blow up and lose my cool!

I then asked Beth this question, *"Beth, what can you ask for?"* She didn't answer me so I told her that she was the most important person outside of the Lord in my life. I told her the answer, *"You can ask for anything, anywhere, at any time.!"* In the days ahead I would often ask Beth, "What can you ask for?" Beth would repeat, "Anything, anywhere, anytime." I wanted Beth to know that I was unconditionally committed to her and that there was nothing that she couldn't ask for. In the days and months ahead, Beth more and more began to ask me for help!

Many nights the only way to keep Beth from itching to the point of bleeding was to gently massage and caress her skin with my fingertips. I was usually praying over her the whole time. One night I came up with a way for us to take our focus off Beth's insomnia and shift to the many blessings that God had bestowed on us."

I gave Beth a hug and said to her, 'Let's pray the ABCs!" Beth was a little puzzled. I suggested that we thank the Lord for something or someone that starts with each letter of the alphabet. We could switch off every letter, A for our daughter-in-law Alex, B for the Bible and Beth, and so on. We luckily had the letter Z covered with our son-in-law, Zach. I never could have imagined the impact of this simple ABC prayer of gratitude in the days ahead. Beth always fell asleep before we got to the letter Z. Oh the power of gratitude in the storms of life!

Our daughter Kristi with her husband Jon had three children ages seven, five, and two, and she was going through the same awful TSW experience as Beth was going through. They lived about ninety minutes away so it was hard for us to be super helpful. My son-in-law Jon was just unbelievable as he daily went to work and did everything he could to support Kristi and take care of his family.

My dear wife Beth, in the midst of almost eighteen months of incessant itching, said to me one day, "I don't want to get better before Kristi!" I already knew what an unbelievable wife and mother she was, but this took my admiration of her to a new level. She wanted to continue with this awful itching until Kristi was feeling better! They were doing the journey together and Beth didn't want to get better first. They were regularly talking on the phone and facetiming multiple times per day. Beth and Kristi were always close, but the TSW drew them even closer.

In the unconscious busyness of this last year, I had joined the John Maxwell Team. I was being mentored online to become a certified leadership coach and speaker. I was taking many leadership classes on the internet. I was hosting my first eight-week Mastermind group for eight people on Tuesday nights. I was so blessed to pour into others as we studied John's book, *The 21 Irrefutable Laws of Leadership*. There was something about serving others in the storms of life where you are blessed more than those you are serving. I think so many people withdraw and look inward when life is challenging.

Both Beth and I continued to attend weekly small group Bible studies. I really think Satan wanted to seclude us and wall us off from others who could support or encourage us during this life. When we joined with other Christians it was amazing how the Holy Spirit ministered to us and through us to others.

I was a member of a Tuesday morning men's breakfast small group called, Iron Men. I couldn't believe how many times I would attend Iron Men after sleeping very little all night, as I supported my dear sweetheart. I would attend looking for the Lord to strengthen me and instead in my weakness, God would not only encourage me but also use me to strengthen and encourage others.

As Beth and I were going through this TSW, we had many people around us find themselves in storms. One of my Iron Men brother's wife passed away. One of my fellow Fight Club brother's wife was diagnosed with vertigo and had to quit her job. They had three children and she was barely able to function. God was using Beth and I to encourage them. As we daily, with the Lord's help tried to have a *live life to the fullest even in the storms of life* attitude we were beginning to realize people were watching us!

January through March was truly some of the most challenging days and nights that we had ever faced. Throughout this eighteen-month journey, Beth and I drank in God's Word every morning and looked to our Lord for strength and encouragement. As I look back in my journal, I am amazed how much encouragement I received from the Word of God.

Yet Beth was really, really struggling. I would stay up most of the night caressing, lightly massaging and moisturizing her. Anything to keep her from scratching. Due to her scratching, she had infections on her face and legs requiring antibiotics. We continued to try to focus on all the things we were thankful for as a way to take our minds off the fierce TSW storm that seemed to grow more intense instead of receding. The ABC prayer became a regular middle of the night ritual.

I was trying to get a leadership coaching and training business off the ground. I was also scheduled to attend the International Maxwell Team Certification Event in Orlando in the middle of

March. Beth was going to get away to Florida and go with me. We looked forward to the vacation, but Beth was feeling so awful I considered canceling!

The fifth ten-week chapter of our men's ministry Fight Club was going to be starting at the end of February. As a squad leader it was definitely an investment of time, but as with many things in life I felt like I often got more out of Fight Club than I gave as a leader. I was trying to recruit men for this growth experience as I was questioning if I should be involved this chapter.

On top of all this, the dentist that I served with on the Romanian mission trip the last three years wanted to split our group into two groups in 2016 so we could reach more people. My concern was that I would then be the lead dentist for a group! What if I had to cancel because of Beth's TSW battle? I was questioning if I should give up on the Leadership Coaching and Training dream and devote all my time to my sweetheart.

In February my dear sweetheart Beth was literally crying a few nights. Understand, my wife never once complained in carrying five babies full term. She was the toughest women I have ever met. Yet she was at her limit. Her beautiful smile that was always there was absent and those eyes that would just sparkle with life, were at times dim.

One morning as we awoke, I asked Beth the question, "What's today?" She kind of looked at me quizzically and didn't answer. I then gave her the answer, "Today is the day you will love me more than yesterday!" As we went to bed that night and prayed, I asked Beth, "What's tomorrow?" Beth answered this time, "The day you will love me more than today!" These morning and evening questions were a gift from God. We started and ended every day with these questions. Beth needed to hear, and I needed to express my unconditional love and adoration!

When I left dentistry and decided to attend the seminary, I had a counseling class taught by a professor who had boys similar in age to my oldest son who was about twelve at the time. This professor told us that when he prayed with his son's before bed he always told them, "I love you no matter what!" From that day on I told all my children "I love you no matter what!" before bed. Years later they would remind me of this. I wanted them to know that I unconditionally loved them. Our loved ones need to regularly hear and feel our unconditional love and commitment!

Rod and Danielle had been living with us for a few months when I could sense Rod was a little antsy. We talked briefly and it was obvious he was struggling with the fact he was thirty-three years old and he and his family were living with his parents. He was struggling with his future being up in the air.

I gave Rod a hug and said, "If Rod I and Rod II can live in the same house for three months with not one cross word between us, I think God has your future under control!" Rod needed to still know that I and his heavenly Father loved him, "No matter what!" It has been over six years since that night. We are so close as father and son and there has never been a cross word since. God has also taken good care of Rod's future!

In late February or early March, I was leading one of the leadership nights and one of the participants asked how Beth was doing. I told them about how I was doing everything I could to just get Beth through the night. I had started a Facebook group so the people in my leadership group could communicate and encourage each other during the week. Nicole messaged me and suggested we listen to a song "Just Be Held" by Casting Crowns. In the days ahead this song became like a theme song of how we learned to deal with the storms of life:

"So when you're on your knees and answers seem so far away, You're not alone, stop holding on and just be held, Your world's not falling apart, it's falling into place, I'm on the throne, stop holding on and just be held, If your eyes are on the storm, you'll wonder if I love you still, But if your eyes are on the cross, You'll know I always have and always will."

There are times in life when all we can do is lie in our Lord's arms and trust him and just rest assured that he loves us and is unconditionally there for us. It was the same with Beth. I tend to be a person who wants to do or say something that will help a situation. She didn't need to hear words or advice from me. All she needed was to lie in my arms knowing there was nothing she couldn't ask for and that I was with her every step, every itch, every scratch.

There is comfort in knowing you are unconditionally loved. When we take our focus off the storm and instead focus on our real strength, a Lord who loved us enough to sacrifice his son, it is amazing the encouragement we can experience. Beth and I needed to learn to just lie in our Lord's loving arms!

So often when people are going through a storm in their life they isolate themselves and find themselves in an emotional downward spiral. We really approached Beth's awful situation differently. My son Rod and his wife Danielle and our beautiful grandchildren— Kaden, age three, and Kallie, age one—had been living with us since late October. Rod was working on his flip house all winter and it was on schedule to go on the market by May.

We continued to watch three other of our grandchildren one day a week while my oldest daughter worked. People often felt our children were imposing on us. Totally not the case! We received immense love and encouragement from being with them. We could focus on our blessings (gratitude), instead of focusing on our difficulties (grumbling).

Nights were just awful for Beth. Itchiness that was truly unbearable. Insomnia even though Beth was dead tired. Her whole body ached. As I reflect on all the things I started to do to support and help my sweetheart, I realize all the ideas were truly answers to prayer from God. I am just not that creative.

In the midst of this, at times almost overwhelming storm, Beth and I after much prayer realized how important it was for me to commit to another chapter of Fight Club as a squad leader. Fight Club kept me focused on where my true help comes from, God and his word and my brothers in Christ.

We also committed to be part of the Romanian mission team. This was a big commitment with the severity of Beth's TSW combined with the fact we were splitting into two mission teams this year. I would now be the lead American dentist of one of the groups. This meant I would have to do all the planning, supply ordering, and I would need to come up with all the surgical instruments we would need. We truly felt God wanted to use us!

During our over thirty years of marriage, we both tended to be fiscally conservative. Beth would discourage me from buying flowers for her. I bought her a dozen roses five times in our marriage, for the births of our five children. Well, I found out you could get a fairly nice bouquet of flowers at the gas station for about $5. I started to regularly buy Beth flowers and with the awful, painful, weary days she was experiencing, it really seemed to raise her spirits when I brought her flowers. I lived to see those green eyes light up!

We attended the International John Maxwell Certification in Orlando for five days in mid-March. Numerous times in the month leading up to this conference I thought about canceling. Beth was feeling so awful. I wondered if it would be best to just stay home. Thank goodness Beth and I were listening to God and not to our weak selves. To be surrounded by thousands of other like-minded people with one desire to serve others and to help others realize their God given potential was very uplifting.

In the midst of Beth's affliction, we stepped out in faith and went to the conference. We had so many opportunities to encourage others. It was amazing how God connected us with people he knew we needed to meet. People who had experienced great personal challenges, physically, relationally, financially, and were reaching out to encourage others.

By chance Beth and I sat at a table and ate dinner with Marie Cosgrove. At the time of this writing, Marie's book, "Greater Fortune" just came out. Marie's mother was raped and chose not to abort Marie. Later as a single mom, Marie was fired by a company. A few years later Marie would buy the company that fired her. Marie's book is an inspiration to anyone who has experienced many storms in their life. God knew our storm was going to intensify so he loving allowed us to meet these people who found purpose because of and in the midst of their life storms.

Beth and I were so blessed to be away, just the two of us. We had devoted the last thirty years to our children and now their children. In spite of Beth's itchiness and weariness, we spent a day at Epcot and just enjoyed the warm climate and each other. We talked about more regularly getting away together. We realized we needed time as a couple to reenergize so we would be better parents, grandparents, and children of God!

REFUGE REFLECTIONS

The words of Casting Crowns' song, "Just Be Held," paints a picture of the importance of where our focus is in the storms of life, *when your eyes are on the storm you wonder if I love you still, but when your eyes are on the cross you know I always have and always will.*

1. The Cross of Jesus is the ultimate picture of unconditional love. Our Heavenly Father sacrificed his sinless son for us, miserable sinners! Are you or a friend or loved one in a life storm? In the midst of this storm, the Lord loves you and is there for you! Reflect on this certainty and rest assured!

2. Do you allow your loving God to wrap his arms around you through regular prayer or time in his Word? Often having Christian music playing at home or in your car will chase Satan away and allow you to feel your loving God's arms around you!

3. Is there someone in your life who is in the midst of a storm and needs to know they can ask you for *anything, anywhere, anytime?*

CHAPTER 8
The Storm Becomes Deadly

The physical reality we were experiencing was that Beth was in constant discomfort. The hotel sheets in Orlando caused her skin to erupt. It must have been the detergent they used to wash the bedding. Beth was going to a wound doctor to help heal infections on her legs. She was dealing with a bladder infection and when we got home from Orlando, Beth went to the doctor, because she was feeling even wearier than she usually felt.

Beth's hemoglobin level was very low. Her hemoglobin was half the normal level. Hemoglobin carries oxygen to the body. If your hemoglobin is low, you will be very tired. In fact, the doctor was amazed that Beth was not more run down. My wife is an amazing woman. She kept on keeping on in spite of her blood count. After a blood infusion treatment in April, her blood counts were still low.

Beth went in for a doctor's appointment and ended up spending over six hours receiving a blood transfusion. This was the entry in Beth's journal that night, "Lord, my day did not go as I would have thought, getting a call to go to the hospital for a seven-hour blood transfusion. I pray that you will help heal me with such low blood counts. Lay your healing hands on me, Lord. I trust that all this is in your plan for you knew what each day will bring long before I was born!" Beth and I were learning to look to the Lord and trust!

A few days later, during one of Beth's sleepless nights, she made a 3:00 a.m. entry in her journal referring to the song "The Potters Hand" by Darlene Zschech. "Lord I am the clay and you are the potter, form me to be what you want me to be. Lord thank you for my TSW! I look forward to using my gift of hospitality this evening with Rod's group of Fight Club men and their wives. Bless that time for all of us tonight!" The next morning, I had a similar entry in my journal thanking God for how the TSW was maturing and completing Beth and I. In the midst of the storm God was accomplishing much in and through us!

We were waiting to see what our doctor suggested next because there had to be a root cause to Beth's low hemoglobin. Transfusions were not a cure. During this time, I found another entry in Beth's journal that really spoke to her total reliance on her dear Lord. Beth wrote, "Lord, I can choose you or I can choose to think about my problems. I choose you! I bring my problems to you and thank you for them because through this TSW I know you will draw me close and make me into the daughter you want me to be!"

Beth was scheduled with a GI specialist in May to see if she had an ulcer. I am a dentist not a doctor, but she didn't have the symptoms of a bleeding ulcer. I also did a little medical research on the internet. At the next appointment with our physician's assistant, I was asking questions and looking for understanding when I asked her, "How do you know it's not cancer!" One thing I was beginning to discover was that some people need an advocate when they are going through health issues. My wife was the most trusting person. She would blindly, no questions asked, follow her health care professional. Little did I know my role as patient advocate was just beginning.

The next day we were fit in at the last minute to the schedule of our family doctor. At our appointment on April 15, our doctor ended up spending almost an hour with us which is unheard of. He ordered a number of blood tests. We had no clue what was ahead, but our doctor was now looking at all the possible reasons for Beth's low hemoglobin. Now we had to wait for the test results to see what was next!

As we were going through all Beth's testing, I was in the midst of my fifth chapter of Fight Club. To be the husband Beth needed, I needed the encouragement and support of my brothers in Christ. Each ten-week chapter we would get weekly assignments in four areas that we desired to grow in: spiritual, physical, intellectual, and relational. If you missed an assignment, you gave yourself one strike. Three strikes and you would not graduate. In my first four chapters of Fight Club, I never received one strike.

Assignments would change from week to week. This certain week in mid-April, one of our physical assignments was to jump rope. Most of the men did not like jumping rope. For some reason jumping rope came easy to me. I had a jump rope session where I didn't trip once and lose the rope from my hand for the entire ten-minute jump session. I was pumped, ten minutes straight!

Well, about a week later, I was looking at the new assignments and I realized that we had instituted something new this chapter. With some exercises, we had two different assignment categories—one assignment for new Fight Club men and a harder assignment for men who had completed previous chapters. I realized that the experienced Fight Club men were supposed to do twelve minutes, not ten minutes, of jumping rope. I had technically not completed the assignment the week before, strike one. I looked back to the week before, another missed assignment, strike two! I was afraid to look at the week before that, but guess what, I had not done the correct assignment, strike three!

I was the first Squad leader to strike out of Fight Club! You could continue to do the assignments in Fight Club until you received a fourth strike. The only thing is you would not graduate or receive a certificate. More often than not, when a Fight Club brother received their third strike, they would drop out of Fight Club. I didn't care. I just wanted to grow as a man of faith. I was committed to keep going and growing.

I wanted one of the men in my squad to step up and become the squad leader, but they all wanted me to continue as the squad leader. It didn't feel right to lead even though I had struck out. But the men had seen my leadership in the last four Fight Club chapters. I continued the last four weeks of Fight Club with the three strikes. So often we don't see the possibilities when things don't turn out the way we want or expect. I ended up being a real blessing and encouragement to the other men who had struck out! I was able to encourage them to keep growing and spiritually fighting for their families!

It was hard to believe but Rod and Danielle and kids had been living with us for six months. Rod's first flip house would be officially sold by the middle of May. My relationship with Rod was growing. As we lived together and as I helped him on his flip house, we began to realize how much alike we were! It was such a blessing to have the smiling faces of Kaden and Kallie in our home each day. They were the perfect medicine for Beth. Next to her faith, Beth's dear family brought her the greatest joy!

On May 5, Beth and I met with a local hematologist. He felt Beth had a type of lymphoma, cancer! It was very hard for us to hear those words. More tests would be needed to confirm his initial diagnosis. At that moment I don't know what Beth was feeling, but I thought we were nearing the end of the awful itching and insomnia of almost two years of TSW, now this. From what we knew, lymphoma was a type of cancer that many people beat!

During the time when we were going through tests and doctor appointments to pin down a diagnosis, Pam, our pastor's wife, texted Beth and asked her if she would like to become the new host for the monthly Young Mom's Night Out group. This was a group of 15–25 young moms who would meet for a dinner prepared for them by the host and then Pam would lead a parenting Bible study. Beth had told me privately for years she really wished she could be the hostess. The woman who had been hosting the group was moving out of state and Beth had her chance. With the new cancer diagnosis, Beth's first reaction was to say no!

Another growth moment for me as a husband. The next morning I called Pam and told her that even with the uncertainty of Beth's cancer diagnosis, Beth was the perfect person to be hostess. Beth had raised five children. She had this quiet, organized strength that the young moms needed to be exposed to. No matter what happened with Beth's cancer and treatment schedule, I asked Pam to reconsider Beth.

I then told Beth, even if I had to prepare the meals and help host, you were born to serve these young moms! Beth would be such a blessing to all the young moms. Her gift of hospitality was only part of the blessing.

A few days later, on Mother's Day, all twenty-one of the Knoerr clan were gathered to celebrate my sweetheart. I remember waking up on Mother's Day profoundly thankful for a woman who was made by God to be a mother, grandmother, amazing wife, and homemaker. I had this sad thought for the first time of wondering how many more Mother's Days I would have to share with Beth. Beth and I were sure emotional in church. Tears were streaming down both our faces. Worshipping God was the place where we always could raise our heads above the surface of the raging waters. We both were so blessed by the songs of praise to the one who gave his life for us!

When we got home from church, I did the hardest thing a father could ever do. I shared with my dear children that their mom had cancer! I will never forget the look on my children's faces as I shared with them. We all joined around Beth and prayed and a close-knit family seemed to grow even closer on that day!

Four days later, on May 12, Beth and I shared a great evening celebrating our thirty-seven years of marriage. We had five happily married children and nine beautiful grandchildren. On our twentieth anniversary, I told Beth that I would "bug" her for fifty more years. If we are to be married seventy years, I would have had to live to be ninety and Beth ninety-two. Seventeen is one third of fifty more years. Since hearing about the possible cancer, I had been praying for healing and would continue to pray every day for such a miracle for my honey Beth!

Chest x-rays, upper and lower GIs, and skin biopsies came back negative. Beth seemed to be sleeping a little better with her TSW and not so much itching. She had a bone marrow biopsy scheduled that would give the doctors a lot more information to arrive at a definitive diagnosis.

While all this was going on, I had been asked to bring the message at our church on May 15, which was Pentecost Sunday. I also had decided to be baptized. I had grown up in a tradition of infant baptism. In spite of all of Beth's health issues, I wanted to profess my faith in my awesome loving God for all to hear and witness.

In my message I used an illustration that Pastor Francis Chan had used in the past. I had a white rope the length of our platform and in the middle of it was about a six-inch section that was colored red. The long, long rope was to represent eternity and the red was our lives. It is so easy to get focused on things of this world like health, wealth, things, frustrations, worries. Yet they are so temporary compared to the eternity we will spend with our Lord because of the death and resurrection of his son, Jesus. Live every day with focus on our eternal salvation, not our momentary struggles.

Wouldn't you know, the night after I shared the message at our church, Beth had a horrendous night. I finally got her to sleep between four and seven a.m. I had prayed for peace in the storm during my first Fight Club two years ago. When I focused on the Lord it was possible to experience peace! It would have been so easy while we were waiting on the final diagnosis to focus only on the negative and forget my baptism day and the privilege I had of sharing the message.

The Friday after I shared the message at church was our Fight Club graduation night, twenty-nine men would graduate. Normally the squad leader is on the stage and hands out the graduation certificates to his men, along with banding them with a leather band. I told our Pastor Kris that I would attend the graduation, but I would not go on the stage with the other squad leaders and graduates because I didn't graduate. This Fight Club was really one of the most moving, enriching, and humbling of all the chapters I had completed.

Beth was suffering more than at any point in our marriage. I really needed the spiritual focus of Fight Club, along with the support of my brothers. Fight Club had been making me the servant husband that Beth deserved and needed. My striking out also allowed me to connect with many of the men at a deeper level. I was just a regular guy that needed the guidance and strength of the Lord. I had no clue how much Beth and I were going to learn how to lean and really depend wholeheartedly on the Lord.

As we were waiting on the final diagnosis, Beth woke up a few days after the Fight Club graduation and told me she was scared! My wife is the most grace-filled, gentle, giving person I have ever met. But she was tough! She carried five babies and never once complained. She just could handle anything. I know it was because of her faith. Beth said she didn't want to be sick so she couldn't play with her grandbabies. I told her that I would do any jobs she needed to do so she could spend every moment possible with the true delights of her life, her grandchildren.

The diagnosis appeared to be multiple myeloma, a bone marrow cancer, not lymphoma. The bone marrow biopsy would determine the severity and treatment needed. We had been waiting almost a month. A little more waiting to go. Ugh! As Beth and I prayed that night, we read John 14:27, "Peace I leave with you, my peace I give to you. I do not give to you as the world gives. Do not let your hearts be troubled. Do not be afraid!"

We had a great family Memorial Day gathering. Obviously, there was this underlying thought in all our minds focused on Beth's cancer. But we focused on our blessings. Living on a lake made for a fun weekend of swimming, fishing, and wakeboarding. What a beautiful family—five married children and nine adorable grandbabies. Cancer diagnosis or not, we were blessed!

Shortly after Beth saw our hometown hematologist, we asked if we could get a second opinion. I didn't know if our hematologist/oncologist would be offended. He welcomed the idea. As our cancer journey moved forward, two things became more and more evident. One, when you are in the storms of life, seek good counsel. I really feel Beth received the best treatment because of the collaboration between the University of Michigan Cancer Center and Dr. Shen, our local oncologist. The second thing that became evident was how important it was for me to be Beth's health care advocate. It was crucial that I ask questions to seek understanding, so Beth and I could be a participant in the decision-making process and not just to blindly follow!

We got up early on June 7 to head to Ann Arbor for our second opinion appointment at the University of Michigan Cancer Center. As I was sitting in the waiting room while Beth was having blood tests done, I looked around the room and realized what a huge role I would play in the process in support of my dear wife. Everywhere you looked there was a bald man or woman. Obviously, the loss of hair was a result of the chemotherapy they had or were receiving. I couldn't imagine what Beth was feeling. All I knew was that she needed to feel love and support from me at a level I had never shown her. Yes, I needed to up my game!

As I sat in that massive waiting area, I thought of the time in the book of Acts, chapter 5, where Jesus's apostles were put in jail for sharing their faith in Jesus. In Acts 5:19–20 it says, "But during the night an angel of the Lord opened the doors of the jail and brought them out. Go stand in the temple courts and tell the people all about this new life." A cancer center has to be one of the most depressing, hopeless places I have ever experienced. I had no clue what was ahead in this cancer process, but I knew God wanted to use us and this cancer journey to tell and show others about our life in Christ.

At 2:00 p.m. we met with the oncologist. She was very compassionate and articulate. We really appreciated how easy she was to communicate with. She informed us that Beth had multiple myeloma, a bone marrow cancer. She proposed a plan of weekly IV chemotherapy with daily oral chemotherapy. Once Beth's cancer numbers were reduced sufficiently, they would remove Beth's bone marrow and treat her marrow. She would then be hospitalized about two weeks, where they would wipe out her bone marrow and immunities with chemotherapy, and then do a transplant of Beth's bone marrow that had been removed from her weeks before.

We had a plan! We were to do the IV chemo in Marshall with Dr. Shen. This would allow us to not spend our life driving to Ann Arbor. We hoped it would allow us to keep living a fairly normal life with our family and church. We would do the two-week chemotherapy/bone marrow transplant at the University of Michigan. There was a lot to take in, but one of the parts of the chemo treatment stopped me dead in my tracks. Beth would have to take a steroid pill on the day of her IV chemo. Steroids!

We were nearing two years in the TSW process and hopefully the beginning of a marked improvement in her itchiness and sleepless nights. Now we were basically going to go backward in the TSW process. We now were faced with not just reading the words but truly trustingly living the words of Proverbs 3:5–6, "Trust in the Lord with all your heart and lean not on your own understanding. In all your ways acknowledge Him and He will make your paths straight."

About an hour after we got home from Ann Arbor, the oncologist from the University of Michigan called. After consulting with her fellow doctors, they felt Beth had the very aggressive form of multiple myeloma called plasma cell leukemia. This is where the cancer in the bone marrow had spread into her blood.

It was very evident as I talked with her that she was very shook. I, with much apprehension, asked her what the prognosis was for plasma cell leukemia. She said at this time there was no cure. The prognosis was 18–24 months! How was I going to break this news to my sweetheart? Dr. Ye wanted to start chemotherapy at Oaklawn immediately. She felt we needed to get to the bone marrow transplant as soon as possible.

That night in my journal I wrote, "Please, Lord, we need a miracle, may Beth and I be the greatest witnesses to the world." Plasma cell leukemia did not have a cure. It could be treated to prolong life but not cured.

As Beth and I got into bed that night I told her, "Don't waste a moment with your grandbabies. I can start grocery shopping or whatever you need for me to give you more time to enjoy our babies!"

Beth also insisted that we do not tell anyone about her prognosis. She did not want anyone to pity her. At the time we didn't realize that by not telling people around us about the short prognosis, we were able to live life to the fullest without others casting a cloud over us. We decided to pray every day for a miracle, live every day for the Lord to the fullest, and let God take care of the rest!

REFUGE REFLECTIONS

1. Have you ever had a time in your life where you were almost to the point of being overwhelmed, yet you felt you could see the end in sight? Then you were slammed even harder by a new storm of life? In those overwhelming moments, Satan all too often gets the upper hand! Or is this the time when our Lord, the Potter, wishes to mold and shape you? A potter, before he can begin to mold and shape the clay, always has to repeatedly beat the clay to make sure there are no air bubbles in the clay. Without beating out the air bubbles the eventual pottery would be flawed!

2. I was the first leader to strike out of Fight Club. I could have retreated in embarrassment. Instead, God used me to encourage other men to stay in Fight Club even though they had struck out! When Beth was diagnosed with cancer, she could have said "no" to hosting the Young Mom's group. Who could have imagined the impact she would have on these young moms in the years ahead!

3. Can you look differently at a season you have experienced or are currently in as a time where our Lord, the Potter, has not forgot you or is not punishing you. Rather he is preparing to mold you and shape you so that he can fill and use you as his wondrous vessel?

CHAPTER 9

Learning to Dance in the Storm

The University of Michigan oncologist quickly communicated with our local doctor and Beth was able to start her first cycle of chemotherapy on Friday, three days later. Beth would have daily oral chemo for three weeks with one day of IV chemo per cycle. She would then get a week break and start another three-week cycle.

I didn't ask Beth what she was thinking as we waited for her to begin chemotherapy. I was praying that the side effects of cancer chemo would be mild for Beth. She had valiantly dealt with almost two years of incessant itchiness and sleepless nights due to the TSW. I was praying the Lord would give her a break. They did give Beth a medication that was supposed to help with nausea.

Beth's first night following IV chemo went quite well. She did not have a sleepless night or experience nausea. I was so thankful of the Lord! As I got up early the next morning before Beth to read from the Bible and to pray, I reflected on a story from John chapter 9. A man blind from birth approached Jesus. His disciples asked if he was blind because he had sinned or his parents had sinned. Jesus said neither of them sinned. Jesus said, "This happened so that the works of God could be displayed in him!"

I wrote Jesus's response in my journal, but I changed the word "him" to "us." I really felt God was going to do great things through us if we but looked to him! The next day, in church a college student who was working for Campus Crusade for Christ, shared the message and he referred to John 9:3 in his message. What an affirmation from God! That was not a coincidence. God wanted to make sure Beth and I were prepared for how he would use us. Little did we know at the time, this verse would become our life verse!

We had been married for thirty-seven years at this point and had seen and experienced a lot of things together, but this cancer journey was uncertainty with a capital U! How bad would the side effects be for Beth? With the TSW, we knew there was an end in sight. We just had to hang in there. Moving forward with cancer, where there was no known cure, is a totally different thing to process and deal with. This made Beth and I cling to each other and to lean on our Lord by drinking in his word and praying each and every day!

Our trip to Florida in February, despite Beth's insomnia and incessant itching, was such a get-away blessing for us that we committed to get away, just the two of us, four times a year. A warm place in the winter, the mission trip to Romania in the summer, and spring and fall weekend trips. Two weeks into Beth's chemo we went to South Haven on Lake Michigan. It was so relaxing and beautiful!

We went to Ann Arbor to meet with the bone marrow transplant team at the University of Michigan Cancer Center. Once Beth's cancer numbers were driven low enough by the chemotherapy at our local hospital, then she would be scheduled for inpatient chemo and the bone marrow transplant at the University of Michigan Cancer Center.

The morning after we went to the University of Michigan Cancer Center, I was up at 5:00 a.m., reading my Bible, praying, and reflecting. I was thinking about my dear wife, the most gentle, grace-filled woman I had ever known. I had left the practice of dentistry for ten years and went to the seminary and served the Lord in full-time church work for seven years. We as a family experienced a number of challenges. My dear wife graciously dealt with all that we faced.

Why did she have to suffer now! Hadn't she suffered enough? This cancer on top of the TSW, just wasn't right! In a weak moment,

I looked at the name of the church engraved on the front of my Bible where we had experienced challenges as a family. That Bible, at that moment, represented the pain my dear wife had experienced. I took the Bible and placed it in the trash can and went to work at the dental office in a neighboring town.

I was about an hour into the day when our receptionist told me that my son needed to see me. It was my oldest son Rod. He and his wife and two beautiful children had been living with us for the last eight months. He shook my hand and said, "Here!" as he handed me a Bible.

Apparently, he had seen the Bible in the trash can and went to the store and bought me a new Bible. He must have felt if the spiritual leader of our family was throwing out his Bible, we were in big trouble. What he didn't know was I was throwing out *that* engraved Bible, not *the Bible*. I needed the Lord more now than ever. In retrospect, I should have donated that Bible to someone who was in need of a Bible.

Two weeks into Beth's chemo our church started a four-week married couples growth ministry called Couples Challenge. We didn't know how atrocious the chemotherapy would be, but Beth and I decided to take part in the Couples Challenge. We felt anything that would strengthen our marriage and our faith was something that could only help us in this uncertain cancer journey. We were to read and discuss a book by Pastor Francis Chan and his wife Lisa entitled "You and Me Forever ... Marriage in Light of Eternity."

In this book, there was a chapter that God knew I needed to read. This chapter truly changed my outlook on Beth's cancer journey. Francis wrote, "I don't have any statistics to prove this, but based on my experience, I'd bet that at least 95% of American Christians would choose not to leave their families today if they were given the choice to be with Jesus in heaven. You can justify that all you want, but something is off. Paul recognized the value of staying on earth to minister to the people around him, but his burning desire was to be with Jesus (Philippians 1:21–26). If you'd rather watch your kids grow up than see the face of your Savior today, you don't grasp the beauty of God. If you worry about what would happen to your children if you were gone, you don't understand the providence of God."

Frances' words were the wake-up call, turning point for me. Once we come to faith, what greater joy could we have than to be with our Savior in heaven. Who was I to say when Beth should leave me and enjoy eternity in heaven! When God wished to take Beth home there would be no more pain or sin or suffering. If I loved Beth as intensely as I thought I did, why would I question God and his timing.

From that day, Beth and I committed to live every day fully for the Lord. I would pray every day for the miracle of healing, but at the same time be ready to rejoice if Beth were called home to heaven before me! Any anger, depression, or disappointment was replaced with the hope of heaven. We could live for him in the power of his resurrection!

Most people, when faced with uncertainty tend to cancel commitments, quit living, and often withdraw from life. That was our first reaction as we tried to prepare for the uncertainty of the cancer chemotherapy journey! My fortieth high school class reunion was in September. I quickly canceled my plans to attend. If Beth's outpatient chemotherapy was effective, she may be ready for her two-week inpatient treatment at the University of Michigan.

We were scheduled to leave on our mission trip to Romania about six weeks after Beth started her cancer treatment. This would be my fourth trip and Beth's third. When Beth's TSW was really acting up, we bought trip insurance in case we had to cancel. Our oncologist definitely did not want Beth to go. He said her immunities would be extremely low and Beth would have a difficult time fighting infections.

This year's mission trip would be different because we split our team into two groups. I was now the only American dentist on one of the teams. Previous years we had two American dentists. Also, our youngest daughter Kristi was joining our team for the first time. After much prayer we decided that we were going to step out in faith, trusting the Lord. If God made it evident that Beth couldn't go, we would reconsider.

Our local oncologist was not happy with our decision. In his professional judgment, he recommended against going on the trip. Apparently, we had told him or his staff we were going to the region of Transylvania in Romania. After we told our doctor that we were still going on the mission trip he often joked about how we were going to see Dracula in Romania!

After prayerfully considering the Romania trip, God seemed to bring us to a realization to keep on keeping on. After listening to God about the mission trip in Romania, we became more trusting of God. In the middle of Beth's first three-week cycle of chemotherapy, she volunteered in the kitchen at the week-long Vacation Bible School at our church. She did wear a mask which at the time felt very conspicuous.

Our seventh annual family pig roast was scheduled for the week before our mission trip. We decided to still host the pig roast. If Beth was ailing, my daughters and daughters-in-law would step up to the plate.

Beth, Kristi, and I went on the mission trip to Romania. Beth wore a mask on the long flights. God was definitely protecting Beth. I unbelievably did not hear one cough on the flight to Romania. We were a blessing to many in Romania. Over 750 people were served and heard the good news of Jesus! I didn't need to ask my daughter Kristi if she was returning. God had grabbed her heart. Beth and I, in the midst of personal uncertainty, were able to be part of a team that was sharing the certainty of our resurrected Lord and Savior.

We were learning to not cancel our involvement based on "if something might happen." Instead, we decided to keep serving the Lord throughout the chemo/cancer journey. We continued to live like we did for the last two years of TSW adversity, even though the cancer diagnosis was considered terminal. The only thing we would end up canceling and not doing was my class reunion. God was definitely teaching us lessons.

July and August proved to be a time where we could either pitch our normal way of life or give in to the life of a family going through cancer treatment and TSW withdrawal. The sleepless nights and itchiness of TSW continued.

We hoped as Beth received a regular steroid pill every week for chemo, eventually her itchiness would improve even though it would reverse the two-year process of ridding her body of the steroids and their effects. No such luck. On top of the TSW sleepless nights, we found out Beth would have one or two sleepless nights related to her weekly steroid pills that she took in conjunction to her IV chemo treatments.

What did our life with a terminal cancer diagnosis look like? We continued to have our son Rod, his wife Danielle, and two children living with us, bringing us great joy and keeping our focus on God's blessings. We weekly watched our daughter Kari's three children on her work day. More blessings to behold. Our children came to our house with our ten grandchildren regularly throughout the summer and enjoyed our house on the lake.

The men's Fight Club ministry and women's Journey Ministry at our church kicked off in August. Beth and I both volunteered again to be part of the leadership. Instead of focusing on the *why* is this happening or the *how* awful will the chemo treatment be or *when* will Beth be called home. We focused on the *who* we could serve and the *what* could we do with the gifts God had given us *where* he had placed us.

As we moved into September, Beth had completed her third cycle of chemotherapy. Tests were being done to determine the effectiveness of the treatment. After evaluating the tests, the University of Michigan doctors were not happy with the response and wanted to switch to a different treatment regimen. Our local oncologist felt switching to a fairly new chemotherapy would be his recommendation.

He made us aware that our Blue Cross insurance may not cover it because the FDA had only provisionally approved it. I wanted him to know where I stood. When your wife is given a prognosis of 18–24 months, obviously you want to stay in the game as long as you can in hope of a "game changer" medication. I asked him, "How much is six more months with your wife worth?" Understand that Beth and I are not wealthy. I told him, "Well, a quarter million dollars is a good start!" He needed to know that I wanted him to consider all options, *all options*, for the treatment of my dear honey!

That night, as we were lying in bed, my dear sweetheart started weeping. She was this amazingly strong woman, who did not often show outward stress. Beth was really struggling with the fact that she had terminal cancer. She didn't say it but she was trying to figure out how to go on living knowing you may be dying soon!

I kept praying that the Lord would make me the support and husband Beth so needed. Beth and my morning scripture and prayer time was so crucial to keeping us focused on the truth of God's word and salvation, not on the uncertainty of the cancer.

I journaled Proverbs 30:5, "Every word of God is flawless, he is a shield to those who take refuge in Him." 2 Corinthians 4:16–18 spoke mightily to me, "Therefore we do not lose heart. Though outwardly we are wasting away, yet inwardly we are being renewed day by day, for our light and momentary troubles are achieving for us an eternal glory that far outweighs them all. So we fix our eyes not on what is seen, but on what is unseen, since what is seen is temporary, but what is unseen is eternal."

A diagnosis of incurable cancer really changes your perspective. I had a totally new appreciation for a simple smile or giving my wife a hug. I would truly drink in those green eyes and smile that caught my eye almost forty years ago. Beth had to have a port placed in her chest so she could receive her chemo through an IV line in the port instead of weekly poking of her arm. For a few days her chest was too painful for me to lie in bed with her in my arms.

The night Beth was finally feeling less pain we peacefully fell asleep in each other arms. So often in our marriage with five children we were moving so fast through life that we truly didn't take time to really appreciate the simple moments. Before we fell asleep, I told Beth, "We are perfect puzzle pieces, we fit together perfectly!" After thirty-seven years of marriage, we fit together not just physically, but spiritually and emotionally. We were on the same page with priorities, faith, family, and friends! It can be so easy to be moving so fast through life that you truly don't take time to really appreciate the simple moments of a hug! No more!

As Beth continued her chemo, we kind of got into a new routine. Due to the weekly steroids as part of Beth's chemo regimen, her itchiness and sleepless nights seemed to be improving. Praise the Lord! We discovered that Beth usually had one or two days of insomnia for each IV chemo. We now expected that. But 3–6 nights with difficulty sleeping in a month was much better than what we had been experiencing for the last two years!

In September we began hosting a weekly small group called "LIGHT" group. I coined the name "Living in God's Hands Together." Our group would be following a book by pastor Greg Finke entitled, "Joining Jesus on His Mission." We were learning how to live our faith and share Jesus at work, at school, in our neighborhoods, at hospitals and clinics. We drew great strength from our friends in this group, as they often were encouraged by us as we met each week to share our lives, pray, and grow.

Both the men's Fight Club ministry and the women's Journey Ministry were going on all fall at our church. We had assignments each week in intellectual, physical, relational, and spiritual. I was totally blown away at the week 2 physical challenge Beth completed while going through chemo. She was amazing! "Keep on keeping on" was becoming our motto.

Beth not only had the gift of hospitality from her mom, Martha, she also had the gift of interior decorating. My beautiful wife, in the midst of her cancer, drew great joy from continuing to decorate our house for every season. I always wondered if our children truly appreciated the seasonal wonderlands that they grew up in. We went from fall décor, to Halloween, to Thanksgiving, Christmas, New Years. Beth would not be Beth if her home was not decorated to accentuate the blessings God showed us at the changing of the seasons and events.

In Fight Club, I had an assignment to look up the meaning of our names. One of the meanings for my name, Rodney, was "famous." Beth's name meant "house." Put them together and you had "famous house." God was really using our house to host—Young Mom's, LIGHT group, pig roasts, and regular family gatherings for his Glory! I was more and more seeing how invigorating it was for Beth spiritually and physically when she would host people in our home in the midst of the terminal cancer storm!

At the end of October, Beth and I joined our daughter Kristi in Grand Rapids where she lived and went wig shopping in preparation for Beth's inpatient chemo, where she would most certainly lose her hair. We had a Harold moment. Harold was my godly father-in-law. He truly cherished his bride for sixty years. We had narrowed down the wig options to two wigs.

I asked Beth to let me surprise her and make the decision. She and Kristi weren't comfortable with me deciding. I then told her that she spoiled my surprise. When my mother-in-law would go coat or dress shopping, she often would often come home with two choices and ask dad which one she should buy. On a number of occasions, his answer was "both!" That is what I told Beth, "You deserve both wigs, sweetheart."

As we were moving toward the New Year, I came across a quote by Corrie Ten Boom that read, "Worry does not empty tomorrow of its sorrows; it empties today of its strength." Because we were blessed with doing Beth's weekly outpatient IV chemo at our hometown Oaklawn Hospital, we were able to intentionally keep on living our normal family and church life.

We were not retreating from life in worry and despair. Instead, we were trusting the Lord and living each day to the fullest in thanksgiving to the Lord for all he had given us! As a response to Thanksgiving Day, I courageously booked flights and a Caribbean cruise for Beth and I right after the New Year. We had always wanted to go on a cruise, but our love and commitment to our family always seemed to get in the way! Go for it, Beth and Rod!

We celebrated a year of Rod, Danielle, and kids living with us. Kaden was now four and Kallie almost two. Rod was working on completing his second flip house. Last year God knew the deadly storm of cancer was going to blow in so he filled our house with love and encouragement. Seeing those beautiful babies every day helped us keep a heart of gratitude for all the blessings we had received from the Lord. Every Tuesday we had my daughter Kari and her husband Zach's three children for the day—Lexi, age eight, Liam, age three, and Landry, age one. Lexi was being homeschooled, so we were blessed to help with her on Tuesdays.

Our son Reid and his wife Alex lived about an hour and a half away and they were expecting our tenth grandchild in June. Our daughter Kristi, who was going through the same TSW withdrawal as Beth for the last two years, was having a horrendous time with fatigue, sleeplessness, and awful itching. Beth and Kristi hit the two-year mark of withdrawal in August.

The awful side effects that Beth had been experiencing began to improve due to the cancer treatment steroids. Thinking the symptoms would be improving, Kristi and Jon decided to have another child. Their family was Calvin, age eight, Caleb, age six, and Charleigh, age three. They were expecting a baby in July of the next year, our eleventh grandchild.

Beth hosted her first Young Mom's monthly dinner two weeks after starting chemotherapy in June. She didn't miss a month. God knew the encouragement, emotionally and spiritually, Beth would receive despite her physical weariness. Beth just glowed each month as she chose menus, shopped, and prepared meals. The young ladies always looked forward to the decorating theme Beth would choose each month. I also looked forward to the chatter of 15-25 young women enjoying each other's company, Beth's food, and, above all growing as women of faith!

As we moved into December, Beth was her normal self, in spite of weekly IV chemotherapy and continuing TSW side effects. She was completing her Christmas shopping and wrapping. She shopped for the Knoerr clan which now totaled twenty people. Each grandchild had the same number of gifts to open, and she somehow was very frugal, shopping 6–12 months ahead, always finding a sale or a deal. Beth always had a checklist, for gift buying, entertaining, you name it. I would fill in the gaps where her life was changed due to the cancer treatment and TSW.

REFUGE REFLECTIONS

1. Spend a moment reflecting on the quote by Corrie Ten Boom that read, "Worry does not empty tomorrow of its sorrows; it empties today of its strength."

2. Are you presently in a storm of life? You may be missing out on the present because you are so focused on questions of the future. It is all about the who, what, when, where, and why, and how!

3. *Why* me? *When* will the storm end? *How* can I figure out a way out of this storm? Satan wins when we ask these questions!

4. You have a choice. Try asking God these questions, *who* can I serve, *what* can I do with the gifts God has given me *where* I presently find myself? You will be amazed the difference in your journey in the storm! When you focus on the *Who What* and *Where*, you will begin to find purpose in the storm!

CHAPTER 10
When It Rains It Pours

At the end of January, after six months of outpatient chemotherapy at Oaklawn Hospital in our hometown of Marshall, Beth's cancer numbers in her blood were reduced to the point she was scheduled for inpatient chemotherapy and a bone marrow transplant at the University of Michigan Cancer Center. No more IV chemo until after her inpatient treatment in January.

The seven-day Caribbean cruise I had booked for early January would work with her treatment schedule. Now was the time, we both were comfortable going for it and living life to the fullest! Beth's immunities, due to the last six months chemo, were low and our doctor did not want us to go on the trip.

I drove to Kentwood to take our daughter Kristi to a doctor's appointment and to watch little Charleigh in mid-December. I came home and told Beth we needed to spend time in Kentwood trying to help Kristi and Jon. Kristi was doing awful. She was two months pregnant, and she was so lethargic with the weariness of TSW, I don't know how she could care for three-year-old Charleigh while the boys were at school.

The next week, Beth spent a few days helping Kristi because she didn't have chemo. We were moving into the cold and flu season. Because of Beth's low immunities, she began wearing a mask around the kids. If they were really sick, we would then avoid them. In spite of Beth's cancer situation, she was a mother first and foremost. She needed to be there for her baby girl and our grandbabies.

A few days later we found out that Kristi and Jon were not having a baby. Kristi had a pregnancy tumor (molar pregnancy). She would be having a D&C (dilation and curettage) to remove the false pregnancy tumor. Wow. The same day Kristi and Jon went into the hospital for the D&C procedure, Beth had numerous appointments at the University of Michigan Cancer Center in preparation for her January inpatient treatment.

There was no way I could begin to have the answers or to in any way help bring a sense of control or direction to Kristi, Jon, Beth, and my lives. "Let go and let God" was becoming more and more a way of life. As God was continuing to break me, I was spending more time with the Lord each morning and throughout the day. I didn't have the answers, but I sure was going to take advantage of spending time with the one who created all things and who indeed had all the answers.

With all our family health issues and challenges, we all came together on Christmas Eve. Our family focused on the ultimate demonstration of God's love, in the birth of his son, Jesus. All twenty-one Knoerrs worshipped together. We spent the day together enjoying our beautiful family at our house, with an amazing day of hors d'oeuvres, dinner, and desserts prepared by Beth. Watching Beth and Kristi, in spite of their health, joyfully preparing for the day was such a blessing to behold.

We continued Beth's tradition that Beth started when our children were young of singing "Happy Birthday" to baby Jesus with a Jesus birthday cake. Many, many gifts were opened. But the high point of the day was when our oldest two grandchildren, both age eight, Calvin and Lexi, with a little help from Caleb, age six, read Luke, chapter 2!

As we approached New Year's Day 2017, my prayer obviously was for a miracle to cure Beth of her cancer or for us to hang in there until a cure was developed. The cancer side effects were nothing compared to her and Kristi's continuing TSW. My prayer was that 2017 would be the year where they both would move past the TSW. As I reflected on 2016 and wrote down goals for 2017, I wrote, "Love Beth, Cherish Beth, Adore Beth!"

January 2, Beth and I were sitting at the airport in Detroit waiting for a flight to Miami where we would board the cruise ship. I was reading the Bible and praying that this cruise would be a time of rest, relaxation, and reflection for us. I also was praying that we would relate with others and share the strength and hope that we had in our faith in the Lord.

Our first cruise day was spent on the ship. It was amazing, great entertainment, food, and above all, Beth had this continual glint in her eyes and smile on her face. We were so blessed to just be together! Our second day was spent on Roatan Island, Honduras. My cancer ridden, TSW challenged, wife snorkeled. There was no way I thought she would want to snorkel. She was truly amazing and so alive!

As we cuddled in bed on the cruise, I started singing a line from the song "Set a Fire" by Will Reagen. "No place I would rather be, No place I would rather be, Here in your love, Here in your love." I changed it slightly and sang the second line, "Here in your arms, Here in your love." Ever since Beth's cancer diagnosis, a hug took on a different meaning. I didn't realize that night how many times in the days ahead I would cuddle my honey and sing those words to her!

So often in the busyness of life a couple hugs in passing. A husband hugs, hoping it's a prelude to something more. I wanted to get the most out of each hug because I didn't know how many hugs I would have. Every evening before falling to sleep and every morning I would hug Beth for a long-extended embrace, the two perfect puzzle pieces that God had brought together.

Recently I read a book by Gary Thomas entitled, "Cherish." He wrote that taking just an extra thirty seconds makes the hug feel qualitatively different. It increases the impact by 100 percent and makes her feel cherished. He said it was not just loving out of obligation, rather cherishing out of delight. He stated that neurologically, hugging releases oxytocin into our brain. Oxytocin, a neuropeptide, is often called the "cuddle chemical" that promises feelings of devotion, trust, and bonding. I couldn't have described it better myself!

While we were on our cruise, our dear daughter Kristi drove to a homeopathic physician in New York to seek help with her TSW. She left New York with some new treatments and hope. We arrived home rested and optimistically looking forward to Beth's inpatient chemo. We were also hopeful that Kristi would soon begin to experience relief after seeing the homeopathic physician.

A couple of days after getting back to Michigan, we received a call from Kristi that dropped Beth and me to our knees. In very rare cases, people that experience the pregnancy tumor that Kristi had, develop cancer. Our baby girl had cancer! No baby and now cancer! Beth and I were more and more relying on the Lord and receiving strength for her challenges, but our daughter having cancer … wow!

The next Monday, Beth would be going to the University of Michigan for four to five daily bone marrow draws that would be treated and transplanted back into her after her inpatient chemotherapy. Kristi was in Grand Rapids receiving her first chemotherapy treatment. It broke our hearts that we could not be with her and Jon, supporting them during this scary time with their three beautiful children.

On the first day of Beth's bone marrow draw procedure another man about our age was there with a supportive friend also going through the same procedure. He was not at peace like us and was really complaining. God gave me the perfect words to help put his life into perspective. I said to him, "Have you ever wanted to be in two places at one time?" He asked, "Why do you ask me that?" I told him, "My wife is here undergoing this bone marrow procedure like you, while our married daughter is having her first day of cancer treatment in Grand Rapids!" I never heard another complaint out of him.

On the fourth and final day of Beth's bone marrow draw, Beth got home and began spiking a fever of 104. We drove the almost two hours back to Ann Arbor to find out Beth would need to be hospitalized. She had a staph infection associated with her chest port. The port would be removed and she was placed on IV antibiotics. With Beth's low immunities they took any infection very seriously.

So much for the plan of Beth starting inpatient chemo at the end of January and Kristi receiving new treatment for her TSW from the physician in New York. Beth's inpatient chemo would be delayed a few weeks and they were afraid the Kristi's new TSW herbal treatment would interfere with her cancer chemo. Right when we thought we knew the plan, everything changed.

God really was drawing Beth and I closer to each other and him. We realized he knew the plan. Why put emotional energy into being frustrated, instead we were praying to see the opportunities in the detour.

Beth was admitted into the hospital on Thursday night. I slept on a foldout cot in Beth's room. In the days ahead, there was not a night that I went home. We were "perfect puzzle pieces." I couldn't get in bed with her but I could fall asleep in a chair next to Beth holding her hand.

There is a saying, "It's not what you are going through that matters, but who you are going through it with that matters!" I adored Beth and she needed to know beyond a shadow of a doubt that amid all the uncertainty I was with her and would never leave her for a second!

The next morning, our senior pastor's wife, Pam, trying to be helpful, canceled the Young Mom's gathering that Beth was scheduled to host on Monday. Pam didn't realize that my organized wife had groceries purchased and meal and dessert planned. The evening went on as planned with my daughter Kari and daughter-in-law Danielle hosting at our home.

We got to know many of the staff in the bone marrow transplant unit who would serve Beth in a few weeks' time. The staff also got to witness our strength in the Lord as they saw our Bibles open every day, praise music playing, and worship services on the TV.

The day after we came home from the five-day stay in the hospital, I was at work and got a phone call from our daughter Kari. She was having a breast lump looked at. She had to have an ultrasound and breast biopsy. At that moment, I will never forget looking up to God and saying, "I do have a three-letter name (Rod). I think it needs to be changed to Job! Little did I know that my younger sister would be diagnosed with a melanoma a few weeks later. Only the Lord could carry all these concerns. I truly was taking to heart the words of Matthew 11:28, "Come to me, all you who are weary and burdened and I will give you rest."

Two days after getting home we hosted our LIGHT small group at our home. We started hosting this group in September. We were studying a resource by Pastor Greg Finke entitled "Joining Jesus on His Mission." We were practicing getting to know people that we would regularly run into in our daily lives. People we saw at the bank, coffee shop, gas station, at work, in our neighborhoods, at school. Simply introducing ourselves and over time having conversations. We were doing simple acts of kindness when possible and when the opportunity arose, sharing our faith!

I never realized how this resource and small group was affecting Beth and my attitude on life. Every day we were getting up not focused on cancer, but on the opportunities we might have and people we would come in contact with as a result of Beth's health challenge. Because of Greg's book and the encouragement of our friends in the LIGHT group and our encouragement of them, we were all becoming more open and comfortable reaching out and relating with people around us.

Over the last few years God had really been breaking me. During my first Fight Club three years ago, I had wanted God to give me "peace in the storm." I didn't have a clue what a storm was back then. As God slowed me down, he was showing me how to look to him and not to rely on my strength. I have learned to experience his peace as I have learned the Lord's strength far surpasses anything I could do.

I was listening to the song, "Praise You in this Storm" by Casting Crowns one morning as I moved into a time of prayer. Wow, I had God's strength and he often gave me a peace only he could give. This strength and peace should result in praise and thanksgiving. I no longer wanted just "peace in the storm." I wanted my response to all God was doing in and through Beth and me to be "praise him in the storm." The Words of Casting Crowns were no longer just words but a way of life we were discovering:

"And I will lift my hands, For you are who you are, No matter where I am, And every tear I've cried, You hold in your hand, You never left my side, And though my heart is torn, I will praise you in this storm"

REFUGE REFLECTIONS

1. Have you ever been experiencing an unbelievable life storm, barely hanging on when you get hit with another life storm? That happened to Beth and me when we got the news of Beth's cancer. During these seasons many people turn their back on the Lord in anger and disappointment!

2. I truly believe many believers coast through life with a ritualistic faith walk where they pray when they think they can't handle it. The rest of the time they don't feel like they really need to spend time with the Lord. Then the storm hits and they lose it. Take a few minutes to look at your life and who is running the show!

3. The only sense Beth and I could make was when we learned to totally surrender to the Lord. It was then and only then that we began to feel peace in the storm. Do you want that peace?

4. As our time with the Lord became more regular it also became more indispensable. Then something happened. We not only felt peace in the storm, we began to praise the Lord in the midst of our storm! For the next thirty days, get up early and spend time with the Lord, reading his word, reflecting, praying, and journaling. You won't believe the difference!

CHAPTER 11

It's Not About Us

The waiting was over. Thursday, February 9, we finally were admitted to the University of Michigan Cancer Center for Beth's inpatient chemo and bone marrow transplant. Our daughter Kristi was about to start her third week of chemo. Beth and my hearts and minds had been focused on Kristi and Jon and their three children. How were we to support them spiritually, emotionally, and physically was the question on our mind.

As Beth began her chemo on the first day, we shifted our thoughts to our 2–3-week stay in the hospital. I had reduced my work schedule to only two days a week so I could be there to support Beth! I only had to work tomorrow and then I would be off until next Wednesday.

Over the first weekend we had many visitors. Our daughter Kristi and her family came. She brought family pictures and decorated our room (in Beth fashion), even the bathroom had Valentine's Day towels. Kristi is so like her mom! You know the saying, "Home is where the heart is!" This hospital room was filled with our love for the Lord, the love of our family, and a ton of family pictures. This was home for a few weeks.

Beth was warned about all the horrendous side effects she would go through. We had gotten to know a number of the nurses from Beth's hospitalization in January. I told one of them on the first day, "We don't participate in side effects!" As a dentist, I had found the value of a positive mental attitude. Whenever I performed an extraction or root canal, the patient always arrived at their appointment prepared for the worst. I spent much time planting positive seeds. In most cases, the patients were amazed at the minimal discomfort they ended up experiencing.

As Beth and I were praying, I said to her, "It's not about us!" The words from John 9:3 about the man who had been born blind again encouraged us, "This happened so the works of God could be displayed through us." These words became our life verse. Every hospital visit, doctor's appointment, anywhere we found ourselves was seen as an opportunity. These words were artistically placed over a wedding picture of Beth and me by our daughter-in-law Danielle.

The bone marrow transplant team members had never met a couple with such a positive attitude. Over the next two weeks Beth did experience sleepless nights from the chemo. Not like we weren't used to nights like this from Beth's TSW. Beth had nausea that was managed by medication, and she only vomited one time. The staff were amazed. Our God, who we relied on mightily, was there to uphold Beth during this time.

Each day Beth was supposed to walk about two miles around and around the bone marrow transplant unit. We obviously took the IV contraption on the walk with us. Many patients were by themselves when they were walking. Beth and I were never apart.

I slept every night on a foldout couch or in the chair next to Beth. Each morning I would go to the family lounge for 1–2 hours at 5:00 a.m. to pray, read God's Word and journal. I didn't want to wake up Beth with the light. I met many people during the two weeks we were there. I was able to connect and encourage fellow cancer patient spouses and staff members.

One of our nurses had an accent and, sure enough, she was from Romania. We shared with her about our four mission trips with the hope of a fifth this summer. One day as Beth and I were walking around the halls, she approached us and wanted to know about the source of our optimism. She had figured out we were people of faith by watching us. She had a friend who lost her 21-year-old son about a year ago and now her friend was diagnosed with cancer. We gave her our contact info and told her we would be praying for her friend Luchia.

Many of the patients were very weak and depressed. Many didn't have someone to walk with them on their daily walks. As Beth and I walked we would notice most of the curtains were pulled over the windows of our fellow patient's rooms. There was such a feeling of hopelessness in the unit.

Beth, in her caring crafty ways, had a plan. She made her two windows into an encouragement. On pink paper she placed our marriage motto, "Living the Dream." Yes, even in a cancer unit we were together living the dream. On a piece of white paper, cut in the shape of a heart, she wrote "Prayer Changes Things."

Beth had our oldest granddaughter Lexi, age eight at the time, make a poster with Joshua 1:9, "Be strong and courageous, do not be afraid, do not be discouraged for the Lord your God will be with you wherever you go." What a powerful verse! When we got, home we attached the little poster to the side of our nightstand. I still look at it every day as I arise and as I go to bed.

Beth made a large pink poster with the words of her favorite Bible verse, Jeremiah 29:11, "For I know the plans I have for you declares the Lord. Plans to prosper you and not to harm you. Plans to give you hope and a future!" Beth also made a large poster that said, "A BIG SHOUT OUT to 7W Staff! Thank You!"

As our two weeks passed, we saw more and more windows opening in the unit and more and more windows with encouragements on them. One patient window had notes, "Love people," "Love is an act of endless forgiveness, a tender look which becomes a habit," "Love One Another," and "Hope is contagious!"

Everyone who entered the family lounge or our room saw us waiting on the Lord with our Bibles open. They could see the reason for our hope. We had many one-on-one conversations with other patients and spouses, and staff.

At the time, I didn't realize why we were daily looking for opportunities. When I looked back in my journals, I realize it was because of our LIGHT small group and the book by Greg Finke, "Joining Jesus on His Mission." What we were learning was becoming a way of life! Greg had a quote in his book that really summed it up, "Does talking with people guarantee something spiritual will happen? No! But not talking with people guarantees that it won't happen!"

When Beth and I were raising our five children, we most

definitely did not make an effort to go out for a regular date night. A number of years ago we were down to our last two sons in the house. One of our sons was in high school and the older son was living home attending a local college.

We were on a one-hour car trip to a funeral home to pay our respects for a cousin's loved one. As we were driving, I told Beth, "Date night!" She laughed at me at first but then we realized how rare it was for the two of us to be out of the house by ourselves with no children or grandchildren.

Fast forward to Valentine's Day 2017. Beth had been receiving outpatient cancer chemotherapy for the last seven months. We were now in the middle of a two-week stay at the University of Michigan Cancer Center. Valentine's Day was always an extra special day for Beth and me. Thirty-nine years earlier I had given Beth her engagement ring on Valentine's Day.

When I realized we would be celebrating this special day at the Cancer Center, I secretly began to make plans for the special day! I went shopping and bought her a beautiful red blouse. Candles were not allowed in the hospital, so I purchased a number of battery-operated votive candles. I purchased a room full of decorations and obviously beautiful flowers. The hospital actually had steak on the menu for the day. I bought nonalcohol wine and two wine glasses.

Those beautiful green eyes just lit up as I gave her the flowers and decorated the room. I helped Beth put on her new red blouse and we sat down at the table in her room with a beautiful steak dinner.

After saying a prayer of thanksgiving to the Lord for the thirty-nine Valentines Days we celebrated together, I had one more surprise. I pulled out my phone where I had downloaded the song that was played for the first dance at our wedding, "You Make Me Feel Brand New" by the Stylistics. The words of that song took us back to our wedding night and brought tears to my sweetheart.

"This song is for you, filled with gratitude and love, God bless you, You make me feel brand new, For God blessed me with you,

You make me feel brand new, I sing this song to you, Make me feel brand new"

For me, this was the most special date we were ever on. It even topped that first Valentine's Day when I gave Beth her engagement ring. How many couples going through the same experience in a cancer ward would have been very negative and instead would have been throwing a major "poor us pity party!" Not us!

In Philippians 4:4 it says, "rejoice in the Lord always and again I say rejoice!" Many people are happy based on the circumstances around them. The best date has to be at an expensive restaurant. Dressing to the hilt is a must. Everything has to be perfect from an earthly perspective. This verse in Philippians has three key words that mean everything, *"in the Lord!"* Joy is a heart concept, a spiritual fruit. Rejoicing has nothing to do with circumstances.

During the writing of this book, my daughter Kari and her husband Zach were visiting with me the night before her hysterectomy surgery. I told them the story about Kari's mom and my most special Valentine's date that was in the cancer ward. I shared with them how I really feel many couples miss out on unbelievable connecting experiences because they are focused on external things like, health, location, etc.

Their three beautiful children would be staying overnight with me and spending the next day with me while Kari had her surgery and Zach was with her. The hospital was about ninety minutes from where we lived. The plan the night before the surgery was for Zach to get Kari settled in her hospital room and then drive home to have dinner with us and to spend time with their three children.

Well, everything went well, and Kari was in her room shortly after lunch. Late afternoon, Zach texted me and said to not wait for him for dinner. A few hours later he let me know he would not be stopping over to see their children. He didn't leave the hospital until about 8:00 p.m. Zach made spending special time with his honey a priority, even if it was in a hospital.

Beth's stay turned out to be fifteen days. She did not require any blood transfusions due to the effects of the chemo and, as bad as it was, it was nothing compared to the side effects we had been warned about! Remember, "We don't participate in side effects!" I honestly believe God wanted us to be available to be a "light in the darkness" and to share encouragement and hope with those around us.

Encouragement from God's Word and prayer were so important, but the support we received from family and friends was unbelievable. I had to work four days while Beth was in the hospital. God in his wisdom and foresight always arranged visitors to spend time with Beth on those days.

Two visitors really come to mind. The first is the son of one of the couples in our weekly small group, Nick. Nick was finishing up his degree at the University of Michigan in April. Because of being away at college, we really didn't know him well at that time. Nick took the time to come up and visit us in the hospital. Many people are afraid to reach out when people have serious health problems. They are afraid of not knowing what to say or saying the wrong thing. So often what they do is nothing. This young man showed a strength of faith and a compassion for us that was just amazing.

The second person that comes to mind is Adrianna. Adrianna originally grew up in Romania and was a coworker of one of the members of our church, John. John told her about our mission team to Romania. Adrianna and her husband decided to be part of our team in July. At the time of Beth's cancer, we had never met them personally. On Beth's last day at the hospital, when I had to be at work, Adrianna came and visited. A total stranger at the time, brought flowers and spent an hour with Beth. She wasn't a total stranger; she was a sister in Christ!

We arrived home at the end of February. After two weeks in the hospital, I started referring to the Cancer Center as "home." Beth and I were together, and we were focused on the Lord. That is home! We had developed many new relationships and friends. But our true home was back in Marshall, closer to our family and our church family.

REFUGE REFLECTIONS

1. Are you in a season or have you been in a season of life where you keep dwelling on the question, "Why me?" How does asking this question over and over make you feel? Does this question energize you or sap the life out of you?

2. Thanks to our LIGHT small group and Greg Finke's book, "Joining Jesus on His Mission," we replaced the "Why me" question with the announcement "It's not about us!" This is a proactive, not a reactive, statement. This statement exudes purpose to the storm we were in!

3. The storms of life blow us into places we never could have imagined. These places can be seen as opportunities that God has provided, not nightmares to wearily endure.

4. Take time to look at the possible opportunities you may have to use your God given gifts in the midst of a life storm!

CHAPTER 12

Praise You in This Storm

We were now home in Marshall, and I could sleep next to my dear wife and cuddle her. Truly the "perfect puzzle pieces" could be back together where we belonged. Beth's outpatient chemo did not result in loss of hair. This was not the case with the inpatient chemo. Four days after getting home I did one of the most humbling things a husband could ever do. Because Beth's hair really started to fall out, I shaved my sweetheart's head. She was so sad! As I went to bed that night, I was praying to God to show me how to more consistently uplift Beth and to make her feel loved and beautiful in my eyes.

The day after this deeply saddening hair shaving experience was Ash Wednesday. We so appreciated this repentant journey every year. As we focused on the Son of God and his journey to the cross for us, so much was put into perspective. The Son of God was tortured, mocked, and ultimately gave his life for us. His mission was to win for us eternal life!

Having this eternal assurance for Beth and me made anything we went through pale in comparison. We considered it a privilege to suffer for the Lord. We were thankful for the different people we were placed in contact with, and we looked for opportunities to share His love.

Beth was still experiencing the itching from the TSW, but it was much improved. She experienced quite a bit of discomfort in her bones, especially her ribs, as her bone marrow was producing new cells after the chemo and bone marrow transplant.

Beth was one tough cookie! But I could tell the days she was weary. She got many compliments on her two wigs. But I know she felt so ugly. Her face was a little puffy due to the steroids. She had put weight on due to not being able to exercise like normal. I kept praying for ways to encourage my beautiful sweetheart.

It had been over a year since I began my morning and evening ritual of asking Beth, "What is today?" where she would answer "The day you love me more than yesterday!" and "What is tomorrow?" Where she would answer, "The day you love me more than today."

I would occasionally ask her if I was a better husband than her dad. A year before she agreed that if I became a better husband than her dad, she would have to shout it from the edge of the fountain in downtown Marshall. These things would put a smile on her face. But she needed more!

For over a year now, I would periodically ask Beth, "What's your name?" She now knew I wouldn't give up until she quietly would answer, "Rod's hottie." I wanted her to know beyond a shadow of a doubt she was the most beautiful woman in the world to me!

One night I felt like I needed to up my game in making Beth feel cherished. Beth and I were both of German descent, so beginning that night, from time to time, I would call her "Hot Grandma" in German. She would just shake her head. I knew inside she was smiling and feeling very cherished.

Every so often when I was cuddling her, I would recount the story of the first night I met her and the one dance we had together. I vividly remembered the blue slacks and red blouse she was wearing, but those beautiful green eyes! Her eyes would just sparkle with life. I lived to see that glint in her eyes.

We still had one or two sleepless nights whenever Beth had her IV chemo. We would regularly say the ABC prayer, where we switched off saying what or who we were thankful for that began with an A, Alex, B, Bible, C … etc.

One night Beth was itchy, she was wearing a scarf so I couldn't see her shaved head, and she couldn't sleep. I started to say a new ABC prayer of thanks but with a twist. Every letter was about my honey. "Lord I am thankful because Beth is "A" adorable, "B" beautiful, bodacious, "C" cute, "D" drop dead gorgeous. Every time I did this, I tried to increase my adjectives of love and appreciation for Beth, "S" sexy, "X" X-rated. Oh, how I got those beautiful green eyes to roll and come alive, even in the midst of her weariness.

In March, a few weeks after Beth got home from the Cancer Center, we had the opportunity to visit East Eckford Community Church. This church had supported our mission team in Romania for the last five years. I would annually report back to the church and give a short message to the congregation.

The pastor had a few people in the church dealing with cancer and he asked if we would share how Beth and I were able to find such strength and hope. To sum up what we had discovered, "Live for today and don't get emotionally weary focusing on the 'what ifs' of the future. Leave the future up to God!"

Three days before we were to go back to the University of Michigan for our six-week post bone marrow transplant appointment, Beth went downstairs in the middle of the night and tripped over a plastic storage container she had gotten out with her Easter decorations. She literally ripped a three-inch by six-inch section of skin off her shin. She still had very low immunities and her chance of infection was great. God was such a provider. One of the people in our weekly small group was a wound physician.

Our six-week post bone marrow transplant appointment went well. After many tests, it was determined that Beth's cancer count was too low to count. She would be scheduled for three cycles of consolidation chemo treatment. At the same time, our daughter Kristi had almost completed her three-month cancer chemo treatment. The doctors felt very good that the cancer was caught early and she was cured.

Because of such good news for Beth and Kristi, I contacted

the leader of our Romanian mission team and Kristi, Beth, and I committed to go on the mission trip in July. Jesus said in Matthew 10:39, "whoever loses their life for my sake will find it!"

More and more Beth and I were learning to not let anything overwhelm us. Instead to bring all concerns to the one who could handle it all. Easter is that ultimate celebration. If our Lord and Savior could suffer and die and then rise from the dead to win for us eternal life, he would be there with us, in every moment, with every concern, with exactly what we needed!

As we moved into May, Kristi was declared to be cancer free and Beth's cancer numbers were too low to count. We were kind of finding a regular rhythm. I had dropped down to working only one day per week as a dentist. This gave me greater flexibility to be there for Beth and to go with her to chemo on her chemo days.

The focus that provided our greatest joy and fulfillment was our family and our church family. Beth continued to host anywhere from 15–25 young moms for the monthly Young Mom's Night Out dinner. As blessed as the young moms were, I think Beth and I were more blessed in the serving. Beth did a special china and crystal Mother's Day celebration. The young moms sure felt spoiled.

May was always a special month. Our wedding anniversary was within days of Mother's Day. Mother's Day was always a special day. My sweetheart, with every fiber of her being, was gifted by God with the personality and gifts to be a mom to five children and their spouses and soon to be ten grandchildren. I was so blessed to be married to the ultimate mom and grandma!

Life in our family wasn't all celebrations. Our 8-year-old granddaughter Lexi needed a second surgery to deal with the infection in her femur. Back to the familiar Mott Children's Hospital at the University of Michigan. Only a couple of floors away from where Beth stayed.

Beth was in the middle of sixteen weeks of outpatient consolidation chemotherapy. There were regular sleepless nights. Also, her immunities were still very low. Life for Beth included regular upper respiratory infections and Kleenex boxes everywhere. My poor baby lived life like normal to most people, but she was an amazingly strong woman dealing with much behind the scenes, and I was there for whatever she needed!

In the middle of May, my sister Vicki, who had surgery for her melanoma skin cancer in February, contacted me and after prayer wondered if she could still become part of our mission team to Romania in July. The answer was yes! My dear wife Beth, my sweet daughter Kristi, and my sister Vicki had all went through cancer treatment over the last few months and they were all responding by saying yes to the Lord and would be traveling in July to Romania to share the good news of the gospel!

A year before in May, Beth was diagnosed with cancer and given eighteen to twenty-four months to live. The twenty-acre abandoned Girl Scout Camp on a lake across the road from us had sold a couple of years ago at auction. It was up for sale again. Just before Beth was diagnosed with cancer we had put an offer to buy the camp and it was rejected. It was now for sale by a different realty company. I asked Beth if we could approach the realtor and make another offer. What couple would consider doing such a thing given Beth's prognosis! Two people who were finding their life by losing their life would do this!

It turned out the new realtor was a fellow follower of Jesus who went to my son-in-law Zach's old church. I put a low cash offer in and guess what, they accepted. By the end of June we owned the camp with an over sixty-year-old building that needed to be totally renovated and was in drastic need of a roof. We didn't know how God was going to use this beautiful property, but we did know it would not be divided up into lots for houses. We were totally trusting that God had a plan.

June 15 marked a year since Beth started chemo. What a fruitful year it had been serving our Lord. We went on a mission trip to Romania and were ready to go on another. Both of us continued to be leaders in our men's and women's ministries. We both continued to attend our weekly men's and women's Bible studies. We continued to host the weekly LIGHT small group in our home where we were continuing to learn and be encouraged to "join Jesus on his mission" in our daily lives. Hospitals and doctor's offices were our new areas to join Jesus on his mission.

I was running three miles in the dark one evening when the occasional house lights and fire flies made me think of how we as followers of Jesus, the true light of the world, were to be glimmers and reflections of Jesus, the Light of the World, in what was often a dark world. What a privilege to serve others and bring the light of Jesus into their lives.

In spite of often wearing masks in public and with family when grandchildren were sick or had colds, we kept living life enjoying the many blessings God had bestowed on us. Mother's Day, Memorial Day weekend, Fourth of July were all regular gatherings at our home,

After Beth was diagnosed with cancer, we finally began to schedule Rod and Beth getaways. We realized the blessing of getting away, just the two of us, four times each year. In the winter either to Florida or a cruise. Spring and fall we would go away for a weekend. This May we went to Holland, Michigan, for their annual Tulip Festival. Our Romania trip was just weeks away.

The weekend before we left for Romania, we hosted the eighth annual Knoerr pig roast. We had 125 people this year. My children were amazing how they helped with this event each year. I think they looked forward to it as much as we did. I again started the pig roast with a prayer of thanksgiving for all that God had bestowed on us over the past year. The tradition continued! Eight years in a row God made sure it didn't rain. I continued the tradition of sleeping in a tent with my grandkids the night before the pig roast. What a great memory and tradition.

We were scheduled to leave for Romania on Friday, five days after the pig roast. Since taking possession of the camp at the end of June with the help of my sons and a few Fight Club brothers, we had torn off three layers of shingles and reroofed the entire roof. All that remained to roof was the roof of a 10 ft x 12 ft room that jutted off the side of the main building.

Two days before we were to leave for Romania, I tore off the roof but didn't have time to get tar paper on the roof. Wouldn't you know that night a storm blew in. I mean it really blew in. It was near midnight and I thought about getting my son who lived a few houses a way to help me try to put a tarp over the unroofed area. I then realized it was so windy that a tarp wouldn't have held.

The old Rod would have been angry with God because the plaster ceiling would now need to be replaced. In the past I would have been thinking, "God I took this big financial risk for you, why are you doing this to me?" But the Rod that God had been breaking reacted in a different way. I pulled up the song by Casting Crowns, "Praise You in This Storm" on my phone. I went outside on our deck, raised my hands to the heavens and sang:

"And I will lift my hands, For you are who you are, No matter where I am, Every tear I've cried, You hold in Your hand, You never left my side, Though my heart is torn, I will praise you in this storm"

I not only had a peace in the storm, I felt led to praise God in the storm. Everything I have comes from him. It was his camp not mine. I just needed to trust the one who created heaven and earth. He knows the future. I ended up completing the roof the afternoon before we left for Romania. God wasn't done allowing me to grow in my surrender and trust. As I was completing the roof, I took my cell phone out and laid it on the roof. That was not a smart move. I hit the phone with my hammer. I needed to rush to the cell phone store that evening. They had the phone I needed, and we were off to Romania the next day.

Often in life our regular routines are interrupted by a life storm and stress, anger, or depression results. People are so focused on the "what ifs" of the future that they miss the blessed God moments of the present. It was almost three years since we started the topical steroid journey and a little over a year since Beth started cancer chemotherapy. Regular routine, what is that? God was teaching us that the most important regular routine should never change. Starting each day in God's Word, praying and reflecting. For me that also included daily journaling.

For the last few months our new routine involved biweekly consolidation chemotherapy. Our morning time with the Lord was often shared as we sat on the ends of our couch looking out at the sun coming up over our lake. This daily routine provided us with a source of strength and peace only God could give. But above all, it gave us perspective.

We were learning to see the blessings in our new cancer treatment life routine. Instead of living life like we were thermometers that rose or dropped based on the environment around us, we were like God, set thermostats. We were more and more able to maintain no matter what was going on around us, because we were empowered and set by our eternal father.

As we boarded the plan for my fifth trip to Romania, Beth's fourth trip, Kristi's second trip, and my sister Vicki's first trip, there was definitely a different feel. A few short months ago all three of them, Beth, my daughter Kristi, and my sister were dealing with a cancer diagnosis. Only God knew that we would all be serving him in Romania months later.

Instead of making decisions in February, March, and April to cancel going, we just prayed and left it up to the Lord. Beth's immunities were still low and her physician did not want her to go. That did not deter my dear wife. What was different this year was that due to the chemo all Beth's childhood vaccinations had been wiped out. She couldn't get revaccinated until August. I could tell Beth was concerned about this. She put it to prayer and was at peace with being part of the team.

Our ten days in Romania were such a blessing. We were scheduled for five clinic days in five different villages. Kristi was able to work alongside her mom doing triage this year.

I am usually the lead dentist for our team. We were blessed to have two Romanian dentists and an American dentist. I was able to be part of the evangelism team this year. I was so humbly blessed. I would ask people if they died tonight, did they know if they would be going to heaven. I can't tell you how many times they would shrug their shoulders. I think they were so guilt-ridden for choices they had made that they didn't think they could do enough good to make up for their wrong doings.

The second day, I kept getting that shrug reaction. I asked my translator, a young man by the name of Emy, how we could help them understand we have been saved by grace, not works. Then I remembered the story of the two malefactors hanging on the cross next to Jesus.

I asked a Romanian man if he knew the story and he said, "Dah," yes in Romanian. I told him there was a difference in the two men. One believed that Jesus was the Messiah. He said, "Dah." I asked him what the Lord said to that man. Then I told him, "Today you will be with me in paradise!" He said, "Dah." I said to him, "He didn't have much time to make up for his sins, did he?"

It was like a light went on in his face. He got it. We are saved by grace alone. Jesus's sacrifice on the cross paid for all our sins. I was able to use this with many people over the course of the five days. God truly does give us the words if we trust and step out in faith.

My dear wife, in the midst of her cancer, was faithfully serving with a mask on when she was working in triage. In 2017, wearing masks made you stick out! As I write this book, so many people are upset about wearing masks during COVID-19. Beth had the choice of wearing a mask and living life, or no mask and a possible life-threatening infection. She chose living! She wore a mask!

I was always looking for ways to encourage my dear wife. Early in the week when I was taking a break, I went to visit my wife and daughter in triage. As I approached Beth and her translator Lumi, something inside of me led me to lean over to Beth's ear and softly ask her, "Are you married?"

Her beautiful green eyes sparkled and rolled as she said, "You better believe I am married!" Her translator Lumi was so blessed by the love she saw between us that day. I did this a couple of more times during the week and Beth's response grew to include how awesome her husband was. I always wanted us to never lose focus of how blessed we were to have each other.

On our last clinic day, we saw our last people in evangelism and I went to the dental clinic to help out. As I was there, I observed that Ken, an American dentist from South Carolina who was new to our team, had an experience I had enjoyed on a number of occasions in my years in the dental clinic.

One of the patients told him he had "golden hands!" Over the years I was told I had "easy hands" or "golden hands." What they were trying to tell Ken was that he had gentle hands. Apparently, many of these villagers often were looked down upon and dentists in the big cities were in a big hurry to deal with them. I was so blessed that Ken, like me, was showing the love of Jesus through his tender care for these dear Romanian people.

Our team saw over 800 people in our five clinic days and gave out over 800 New Testament Romanian Bibles. I personally was also able to share the message in two different churches while in Romania. Often when people are experiencing a storm in their life they wall off and retreat. Like Samuel in the Old Testament, my dear wife, daughter, and sister, responded to their health challenges by saying, "here I am, send me!"

With Beth's terminal cancer diagnosis, we decided to take a side trip on the way back from Romania. We spent three days in Germany on the way home. The year 2017 was the 500th anniversary of the Reformation when Martin Luther nailed the 95 Theses on the door of the Castle Church in Wittenberg, Germany. Beth and I have a German heritage so it was a real blessing to see the country that our grandparents and great-grandparents emigrated from, along with physically visiting this historic town of Wittenberg.

We returned back home from Romania very blessed, but back to the real world of our lives. Beth would be having a bone marrow biopsy to determine how her cancer had responded to her inpatient cancer treatment and the follow-up consolidation chemotherapy. I had only been working one day a week as a dentist so I could, first of all, support Beth. After much prayer we decided that I should explore new opportunities to work more as a dentist when we returned from Romania. Working one day per week was not paying the bills.

REFUGE REFLECTIONS

1. When life storms blow in do you see them as an inconvenience you must endure until you can get back to your normal routine? Are you growing weary trying to keep up your routine even in the midst of the raging storm?

2. Beth and I discovered over the now three years of TSW/cancer storm that our life needed to be downsized. The storm helped us prioritize what was important. With limited time and energy, God was showing us how best to use our limited time and energy! How do you need to better prioritize?

3. Take time to step back, wait on God, and prayerfully consider a new routine. I am writing during the pandemic. In the beginning everyone wanted to go back to normal. Now almost two years in, the storm of the pandemic has forced people to live differently and discover a "new normal!"

4. As Beth and I more and more looked to the Lord to show us a more simplified life routine, we moved from not just experiencing peace in the storm to actually "praising" the Lord in the storm! The storms of life are your opportunity to discover a new normal. Don't waste your storm!

CHAPTER 13

Eye of the Storm

After getting back from our mission trip to Romania, I went into the dental office where I had been working for over four years and mentioned to the office manager that I was going to be looking for additional employment. She pulled me aside and let me know they had been interviewing young dentists. The doctor's hope was to find a dentist that could eventually take over for him when he retired. When I started working for him almost four years ago, I knew this would eventually happen so I understood, but it was a shock!

This news was balanced by the results of Beth's bone marrow biopsy. My sweetheart was declared cancer free and in remission. Praise to the Lord! We had a visit with our oncologist at the University of Michigan and she was explaining to us the recommendations for Beth's cancer remission maintenance chemo. Beth would continue on a reduced chemotherapy, but for now her cancer was not active. She asked if we had any questions or concerns.

Obviously, I had a concern! In my off-the-wall normal self, I told her that due to Beth's chemotherapy I was having to make some adjustments after almost forty years of marriage. She looked at me with a very concerned look and asked me what was going on?

I told the doctor that for the first time in almost forty years of marriage I was married to a "curly girly! She looked at me with a puzzled look. When Beth's hair started growing back, it was curly. Beth looked so cute in her "curly girly" new look!

The morning after we got the great "no cancer" news, I cuddled Beth for almost two hours. As much as we prayed for a miracle of healing every day, a simple cuddle or hug had taken on a whole new meaning when you wonder how many hugs you will get! I treasured every moment, smile, and just plain time together. As I looked at the choices we had made on how to live life over the last few years, I realized it was because of our daily focus on the Lord in prayer and reading his Word. Together we chose to live for today and not wear out our brains with the "what ifs" of the future!

Beth and I went on one of our four times per year getaway trips to South Haven on Lake Michigan and then threw ourselves into life. We were now celebrating a year of hosting our Thursday night LIGHT (Living in God's Hands Together) group. We all were really growing in our ability to "join Jesus on his mission" in our routine day-to-day encounters.

The seventh chapter of our men's ministry Fight Club was scheduled to start in September. I was again a squad leader for this amazing ministry. Fight Club was a lot of work and commitment for ten weeks. In fact, not a chapter went by where I didn't seriously consider dropping out. Satan would do everything he could to wall me off from others and from the Lord. I needed this focus on the Lord and the fellowship of my Fight Club brothers!

Every Tuesday morning, I continued to attend the Iron Men Bible breakfast gathering at 6:00 a.m. Most of the men were much older than me. In fact, over the last year two of them had their wives pass away. I so appreciated hearing about their life experiences and discussions.

While Beth and I were beginning to start another "new normal" routine with her maintenance chemo, I was transitioning out of my four-year dental job in one office, substituting in offices in metro Detroit and eventually, in November I started a dentist job four days per week in a corporate-owned clinic in a town near where we lived.

Nothing was routine when working in many different dental offices. My faith and my love of serving my patients was where I put my focus. Sometimes in life things around us are chaotic and not routine. It is then that we need to focus on our faith and the unconditional love and presence of our Lord. Focusing on our Lord allowed me to more and more find a sense of calm in the choppy, daily storms of life.

My son Rod had completed and sold his second flip house and was soon to start on another house. After getting back from Romania we really began the renovation of the camp building. We were replacing rotted siding, installing all new doors and windows, and painting the entire exterior.

God was truly using this camp as a way to bond Rod and I together after so many years of us being separated and estranged. The more we worked alongside each other the more we realized how alike we were. I would go to give him directions on what to do, and he was already thinking about doing the same exact thing. He also would approach different renovation situations in the exact same way as I would have suggested.

Our oldest granddaughter Lexi, age nine, loved coming out and helping in any way she could at the camp—pulling nails out of boards so we could burn up the boards, raking leaves, sweeping up debris. She was so blessed to help. I told her one day God would use her as we seek God's plan on how he would use the camp for his glory.

In October Rod and his four-year-old son, Kaden, and I constructed a life-size cross of Christ. At our mid-chapter Fight Club midnight gathering I had a special plan to use the cross. Each of us Fight Club brothers took turns carrying/dragging the cross around the trails of the camp in the dark. What a moving time. It was difficult enough for each of us to drag the cross.

Imagine our dear Savior, after being whipped and flogged, trying to drag the cross toward Calvary. Oh, how Jesus loved us! At the end of our dragging, I had already dug the hole. In a very solemn, memorable moment, all of us men placed the cross into the ground. This was the first use of the camp since we purchased it in June. Praise the Lord!

During this fall and early winter, Beth was being Beth. Our five married children and ten grandchildren all lived in Michigan. Three of the married children and five grandchildren lived near us in Marshall. The other two families were less than two hours away. Our house could best be described as a bed-and-breakfast, just the way Beth loved it. Beth was always hosting a special family gathering—Memorial Day weekend on our lake, Halloween, Thanksgiving, Christmas. This amazing woman Christmas shopped for our family of twenty-two. Her great joy was hosting, cooking, and giving gifts to those she loved. Beth again was the organizer and host for our church Thanksgiving Dinner for around 300 people.

But there continued to be what people didn't see about Beth's life. Beth's reactions to chemo varied but were usually insomnia, sometimes chills or nausea. With less chemo treatments she was getting less steroids and her skin itchiness was returning. Beth had almost continuous upper respiratory infections and urinary tract infections in October. She got a new chemo port in her chest in November and had a fever. Luckily, antibiotics worked and she didn't need to be hospitalized.

We usually had our oldest daughter Kari and her husband Zach's three children one day a week. What a blessing! Our oldest son and his wife with their now five- and two-year-olds, were coming up on two years living with us also. So many people commented to us that Rod, Danielle, and their kids must be such a burden for us. They moved in about six months before Beth's cancer diagnosis.

We had been watching Kari and Zach's kids one or two days a week for over eight years. How many people would have thought the cancer was all they could deal with and would quit babysitting and miss out on God's blessings. Same with Rod and Danielle living with us. God knew exactly what he was doing. They were a blessing to us and we sure were a blessing to them.

At the end of November, Beth, our daughter Kristi, and I mailed in our registration to be part of the Romania mission trip in 2018. This would be my seventh trip, Beth's sixth trip, and Kristi's third trip.

We decided to host our family Christmas gathering out at the camp. It was not completely renovated and did not have a furnace system yet, but Beth was determined for our family to gather at the camp. We used a temporary heater, and her decorating made the camp a special place to celebrate the birth of our Savior. Beth was so in her element as we cleaned up the camp and decorated! Her spiritual gift was most definitely hospitality.

Four days after Christmas Beth woke up with extreme abdominal pain. Off to the ER we went at 6:00 a.m. Wouldn't you know, Beth had a kidney stone. She did pass the stone and, praise the Lord, was much more comfortable by the next morning. As I reflect back on our reaction to Beth's kidney stone, I was more and more realizing that when we were the weakest, God's strength was truly sufficient.

Beth's mom's side of the family had a tradition of making a big deal out of New Year's Eve. Her extended family—aunts, uncles, and cousins—always gathered. The countdown to midnight culminated with hugs and kisses to usher in the new year. The family gathering was her family's way of recognizing and thanking God for all his blessings. This year Beth and I quietly rang in the New Year by ourselves as we hugged and kissed. I wrote in my journal, "2018 is about Beth and my legacy."

At the first Young Mom's Night Out gathering of 2018, Beth started the tradition of having each mom pick a "Word for the Year." Beth provided small canvasses and paint supplies so each mom could artistically accent their word for the year. With everything Beth had endured with the Lord's strength, she chose the word JOY for 2018!

For many years, one of my favorite portions of Scripture had been Philippians 4:4–7. The apostle Paul wrote this letter of encouragement to the people of Philippi and to us from prison. "Rejoice in the Lord always, and again I say rejoice!" says Paul in verse 4. He didn't just say rejoice when things were going well. He said "always." Then he repeated himself, "And again I say rejoice!"

Less than six weeks after starting to work in this dental office, I was written up by the head of Human Resources for supposedly "talking about my faith." I really dislike when people are pushy about their faith. I always made a point in my dental career to never talk about my faith with a patient unless the patient was already talking about their faith.

The Human Resources head also wrote me up for "making patients uncomfortable talking about my wife's cancer." Again, only when a patient was telling me about themselves or a loved one going through cancer, did I try to encourage them by sharing our cancer experience. I believe it was not a patient but a coworker who made these accusations. At the time I was pretty upset because they would not remove these accusations off my record. I finally had to surrender and realized I was getting a lesson in taking up my cross and following the Lord!

Our circumstances in many cases will not lead us to feelings of joy. Yet, when we look at the innocent Son of God being tortured and crucified for our sins, we are amazed at such love. Any cross that Beth and I had to take up and carry was nothing compared to the cross of Jesus. For this we would always have reason to rejoice. We entered 2018 not discussing, but I am sure we were both inwardly thinking about Beth's prognosis of 18–24 months to live. January marked twenty months since Beth had been diagnosed with cancer.

In July 2016 I had been serving in the dental clinic in a small village in Romania when a young man named Eric walked up to me and said "Go Blue!" I am a University of Michigan School of Dentistry grad and saying "Go Blue" is a way to call attention to a common allegiance to the University of Michigan. The leader of our mission team, Steve was an Ohio State grad. His alma mater was the chief rival of my school, the University of Michigan. Apparently, Steve had made Eric aware of the fact I was a University of Michigan alumnus.

It turns out Eric was a Michigan fan and had grown up in the United States and had married Lily, a Romanian young lady. Eric was now living in Romania and involved in ministry. Our mission team had representatives from at least five states. Eric asked me where I was from. I told him Michigan. When I told him the city of Marshall, we discovered he grew up about ten miles from where Beth and I lived. What a small world! This also explains why he was an avid University of Michigan sports fan.

In January, Eric, his wife, and three beautiful children were in Michigan visiting family and we were able to host his family for dinner one evening. Who would have thought a couple country boys from Michigan would meet in Romania doing the Lord's work? God knew and now he allowed our families to meet. What a cause for rejoicing. God had a purpose for allowing us two brothers in Christ to meet! My oldest granddaughter Lexi and Eric's oldest daughter Ruthie connected that night. How cool.

During this winter season we definitely found reasons for rejoicing as we worshipped at our church each week. I noticed that Beth was more and more raising her hands in praise. Beth was not an outwardly demonstrative person and she grew up in a very conservative church. Yet, as the storms of TSW and cancer would not relent, Beth's focus and love for her Lord and Savior grew and grew. The woman with terminal cancer was in the third row of church with her hands raised the highest to her Lord! God was majorly feeding us through the preached Word, worship time, and with the support and fellowship of our dear friends in Christ.

Philippians 4:5–6 says, "Let your gentleness be evident to all the Lord is near. Do not be anxious about anything, but in every situation, by prayer and petition, with thanksgiving, present your requests to God. And the peace of God that transcends all understanding, will guard your hearts and your minds in Christ Jesus." Beth was in remission, but every two weeks she would have 1–2 nights of insomnia. She was constantly dealing with an upper respiratory infection and would occasionally spike a fever. There was always a worry of significant infections due to her low immunities. Most people were not aware of what Beth dealt with on a regular basis as we, for the most part, lived our life with our large family quite normally.

In February, dear friends from our church who were in our weekly small group, treated us to a Steven Curtis Chapman concert. Steven is a Christian singer. He and his family were definitely acquainted with following the Lord and trusting him for strength and peace in the times of adversity and the storms of life. A number of years ago their son was pulling in the driveway and ran over his little sister. That was the day Steven's daughter opened her eyes in heaven.

So many people have blessed us during Beth's difficult health care journey. I know people don't know what to say or how to react when people they know are going through the storms of life. It isn't what you say. It is the fact you care! We too were finding out, when the Spirit is nudging you, go and connect and encourage. We, like our dear friends, trusted God to give us the words.

Our dear friends had no clue how much we loved Steven Curtis Chapman. In a ridiculous leap of faith to most of my family and friends, I left my dental practice after only eight years of practicing dentistry to attend seminary. Our four children were between the ages of three and ten. In 1999, after having moved many times, we were part of starting a new church. At the church service to install me as the official pastor, my family and I chose to sing the song, "For the Sake of the Call" by Steven Curtis Chapman. By now we had five children who now ranged between five and seventeen. The words of this song had such great meaning for Beth and I as we tried to live for Christ. We were in the front row at this concert and Steven sang these words ...

"We will abandon it all for the sake of the call, No other reason at all but the sake of the call, Wholly devoted to live and to die for the sake of the call"

If you have never heard this song, you need to hear the entire song. If I were to pick a song to best represent Beth and my marriage it would be this song. When we were dating, the plan was to move back to Beth's hometown of Saginaw, Michigan, near her parents. My parents lived in the neighboring city. We wanted to set up a dental practice, serve the Lord, and have a big family. No thoughts of moving anywhere. Answering Jesus's call resulted in us living in sixteen different places, owning nine different homes. One reason ... the call! Even in the storms of life we were living in abandon "for the sake of the call!"

My oldest son and I were working on renovating and painting the inside of our camp building. Two and a half years ago Rod and Danielle and the kids, in the middle of a life storm, moved in with us. God began to help Rod and I discover a relationship we had never experienced or dreamed was possible. Beth and I acted in reckless abandon, like the disciples, and bought the camp last year.

We were excited to see how God would use this camp for his purposes in the years ahead. But the renovation of the camp was God's ultimate gift to renovate my relationship with Rod. We had now lived in the same house for almost two and a half years. We now have a respectful, loving adult father/son friendship and appreciation for each other!

We were working hard to get the inside of the building to the point that we could host a neighborhood Easter gathering in the building. There was much to complete, but Rod and I were able to get the large gathering room cleared enough to accommodate an Easter gathering. We passed out flyers and invited neighbors.

About thirty people attended our Easter celebration at the camp. Beth and I were so blessed to hear Calvin, our ten-year-old grandson read the Easter story from the Bible. His mom, my daughter Kristi, accompanied our singing on the keyboard and did a children's message. When Beth and I purchased the camp a year after she was diagnosed with cancer, we knew that God had a plan for this camp. Easter gave us another glimmer of how it could be used!

Shortly after Easter my son Rod and his wife Danielle informed us that they would be moving out. Rod had accepted a job across the state about two and a half hours away. It was time for them to move on in their marriage with their family! We had so many mixed emotions. God had done a great work in drawing Rod and I together. Their family was the exact medicine we needed as we walked through Beth's health storms!

Around that same time, I was in church worshipping, when God gave me this overwhelming conviction that Beth was cured! It was like something I had never experienced. I told Beth about what I had felt. I encouraged Beth to go to the Lord in prayer and seek him. I had prayed every day for a miracle cure for Beth for almost two years! God can do it! A few weeks later Beth told me she wanted to discontinue her chemotherapy treatment. How do you know if you are cured if you keep taking chemotherapy during remission?

REFUGE REFLECTIONS

1. Are you open to major life commitments when you are being
    battered by the winds and waves of life's storms or have you
    decided to hunker down and separate yourself from the
    world until the storm passes?

2. A year into Beth's horrendous TSW, we invited our son, his
    wife, and two grandchildren, ages one and three, to move
    in with us. Eighteen months later, one year into a terminal
    cancer diagnosis, we took a leap of faith and purchased the
    camp! This made no sense I am sure to those around us.

3. Why did we do these things? To most people our decision
    looked sudden and ill planned. People didn't know that
    while Rod was estranged from us for over two years, Beth
    and I had been praying every day for a person or an event to
    come into Rod's life. Ever since going to Romania in 2013
    I had been praying, asking God how and if he wanted Beth
    and I to purchase the camp for his use. After four years of
    prayer, we purchased the camp.

4. Do you have a regular daily time where you spend time with
    the Lord? I truly believe Beth and I were totally at peace in
    the midst of the storm when we made the decision to have
    Rod's family move in with us and purchase of the camp.

5. God may have opportunities before you that are obscured by the waves and winds. Today is the day to begin spending time with the one who clearly sees your future and wishes to show you!

6. Beth's verse says it all, Jerimiah 29:11, "I know the plans I have for you declares the Lord, plans to prosper you and not to harm you, plans to give you hope and a future!" Often the Lord shows us those plans and opportunities in the midst of the storm. Is he trying to show you a way through the storm into the future, but you aren't spending time with him? Today is the day to start!

CHAPTER 14

Choppy Calm Before the Storm

In the middle of April, we had great reason to celebrate. Our dear daughter Kristi was declared cancer free for one year. Praise the Lord! She was looking forward to her third mission trip to Romania in July. This would also be the third year since Beth's cancer treatment began that she would boldly share her faith in Romania.

After much prayer by Beth, at her first appointment in May with Dr. Shen, her oncologist, she informed him that she wanted to discontinue chemotherapy. Beth had been in remission for eight months. She basically told him, "How will I know if I have been cured as long as I continue a maintenance chemo during my remission?" Dr. Shen did not try to convince Beth to the contrary.

We were blessed to have the Romanian pastor and his wife, Jon and Ani, visit us in early May. Their son Flavius had assisted and served as translator for us dentists on many mission trips. From that experience, he had decided to become a dentist. He was graduating with his bachelor's degree from Calvin University here in Grand Rapids, Michigan. He would be starting dental school in Pennsylvania in the fall. It was such a blessing to spend a few days with Jon and Ani.

We spent a day and drove down to Kentucky to visit the Noah's Ark exhibit. With my ever-changing job situation and Beth's years of health challenges, we were better prepared for the unexpected things that Satan threw at us. About an hour north of the Noah's Ark exhibit, we stopped to get gas. When I tried to start our minivan, it would not start. If we spent too much time trying to get help, we would have wasted the three-hour trip to Kentucky.

My van was quite old. I very quickly was able to rent a car nearby. I also called a car salvage place and arranged for them to pick up my old van. I left the title in the van and the keys with the gas station. We only lost an hour of our day. To see and to walk through a full-size replica of the Ark gave us a greater appreciation of the power of our Lord and the faithfulness of Noah and his family!

While Jon and Ani were in the US, we gathered at the camp with the six people from our church that were going on their first mission trip to Romania. Our friends from our LIGHT small group also joined us for a great evening of fellowship, encouragement, and prayer. It was so moving when we all knelt in a circle and took turns raising up prayers to the Lord.

When I went down to working one day each week in April 2017, I wanted to spend every possible moment with Beth. I prayed that God would do a miracle every day and cure her, but reality was that she was given 18–24 months to live. If God called Beth home, I would have plenty of time to work and pay bills.

When Beth was declared to be in cancer remission in August, I felt God wanted me caring for patients and generating income. I started working four days per week in November for a corporate owned dental office. The great plus about this office was that it was located literally fifteen minutes from our home. I would not be spending a lot of time driving to work and back away from Beth!

Back working as a dentist at first really energized me. I was able to connect with patients and show them God's grace through my clinical skills and more profoundly through personally connecting with them. I also had the opportunity to mentor a young man who was just out of dental school.

After a couple of months of working in this office I was asked by the head of Human Resources if I would substitute two days a week in another dental office. I am always a team player, but my concern was that the office was over an hour drive away from our home. I didn't know how many days or years I had left with Beth, but I didn't want to waste any. Yet I understood this office had just lost a dentist and they were doing their best to take care of the needs of their patients.

Over the previous few months, I had been trying to observe the exhortation of the apostle Paul in Philippians 1:6 where it said, "In every situation, by prayer and petition, with thanksgiving, present your requests to God." After much prayer I agreed to the hour drive to substitute in the other clinic.

It was hard to commit almost two hours each day driving to work and back when you don't know how long your wife will be on this earth. A few weeks after I started substituting, I was asked to work four days per week in this office. The new dentist would not be arriving till the middle of June—six whole weeks!

In the two weeks I had worked there I was so blessed by the staff in that office. One day shortly after I started in this office, I was doing an exam on a young mom. She told me how, while she was pregnant with her one-year-old daughter, her husband was diagnosed with cancer.

I was able to share with this young woman how our faith had been our strength during Beth's cancer journey. This couple also knew the Lord. She was so appreciative and encouraged that I took the time to share about Beth's cancer journey and the strength we were receiving from the Lord. This interaction emboldened me to "Not be ashamed of the Gospel" as it says in Romans 1:16. Beth and I continued to discover, the places we found ourselves, and people we had come in contact with due to her health challenges, opened doors of opportunities for us to encourage others!

I was counting the days till I wouldn't be spending two hours driving to work and back away from my sweetheart! When the new dentist arrived, instead of returning to the office I had worked at that was fifteen minutes from my home, I was given the opportunity to work in another office that was also almost an hour from my home.

I was very disappointed and really frustrated, but through our journey God was beginning to teach me how to "pray first and speak second." After prayer with Beth, I agreed to start in this office a couple weeks before we would leave for our mission trip to Romania at the end of July. I needed to "let go and let God" as the saying goes. This definitely applied to how we were approaching Beth's cancer journey.

Too much of my life I had exerted tons of emotional energy when I should have knelt in prayer and trusted God to act in his time. I needed to look to the Lord who gave up everything so that I could be saved! It was my opportunity to take up my cross and follow Him! True hope and peace would only be found when I trusted and followed!

During these months that I was spending so much time driving to work and back, we outwardly led a pretty normal Rod and Beth life. Beth continued to have low immunities due to her maintenance chemotherapy. In order for us to keep on keeping on, Beth wore a mask in public. At the time of my writing of this book, I have to chuckle because we are in the midst of the COVID pandemic and everyone is wearing masks!

Beth was one of those people who loved to stay out of the limelight and faithfully serve the Lord under the radar. She initially felt the mask drew attention to her and she didn't like that. But she realized she wanted to live life to the fullest with our family and friends and she wanted to serve the Lord with the gifts God had given her, so she wore the mask.

We never missed Sunday worship, we continued to host our weekly "joining Jesus on his mission" LIGHT group every Thursday. Beth attended a Wednesday morning women's Bible study. The highlight of each month was hosting and making dinner for the young moms of our church. The joy and laughter of those 15–20 young mom's as they enjoyed Beth's meal and each other's company was such a blessing to Beth.

Then there were all the activities of having five married children and at that time ten grandchildren under the age of ten. Beth continued to regularly watch three of our grandchildren one day each week as my daughter worked as a dental hygienist. After two and a half years our son and daughter-in-law moved out of town. Their children were now three- and five-years-old when they moved out in May.

Beth was constantly dealing with an upper respiratory infection. Often, she would have a urinary tract infection. Her one knee was in need of a new knee replacement, but with her low immunities they were not willing to do the surgery. Beth wore a knee brace and just endured! Out of nowhere Beth began to experience blurred vision in her right eye. It turned out to be a broken blood vessel and eventually resolved itself.

We found if we focused on our blessings, it took our focus off my job and her cancer journey. As a couple we regularly prayed and God more and more allowed us to trust him as we spiritually would lie in his arms. We have a painting in our living room with the words of Psalm 46:10, "Be still and know that I am God." Our Lord truly does bring that peace and stillness in the midst of the storms of life.

Almost every entry in Beth's daily journal in 2018 involved thanksgiving to the Lord. She even ran through the alphabet a few times with a different blessing that started with the letters of the alphabet. She over and over and over raised me and my job situation up in prayer. I really think God had her focused on my storm at work so it would take her focus off her storm of terminal cancer!

In May we got away for a long weekend and went to South Haven on Lake Michigan to celebrate our thirty-ninth anniversary. We had been so blessed by the Lord. Mother's Day was the day after our anniversary, just like the year we were married. I think Satan slyly convinces people to withdraw during the storms of life. Satan is good at making people feel like they just don't have the energy to do things. We refused to listen to Satan!

Warm weather in Michigan is basically June–August each year. We Michiganders live nine months looking forward to summer. Our lake home would really be a bed-and-breakfast for the next three months with our large family and we wouldn't want it any other way.

I saw this entry in Beth's journal at the beginning of June, "My job is to reflect your glory, Lord. Help me to stay focused on you, the giver of life!" As we moved along in this cancer journey, I more and more realized that my greatest joy was assisting Beth as she used her gifts. Seeing her beautiful green eyes light up with excitement as she was serving others was her way of reflecting the Lord's glory!

Like Beth with her cancer, I needed to live each day serving the Lord, letting my light shine. God had the future figured out and I didn't need to worry! I had no clue what the future would bring, but God did! Just relax and trust! If I had not finally let go, I would never have recognized all the blessings of that two months of substituting in the office where I was on the road almost two hours each day. I wonder how often when people are going through the storms of life and are so focused on what they think the answer should be that they miss out on the blessings in the storm.

I was getting settled in at the new dental office. It seemed like there was a talented staff. The office had lost two dentists recently, so I was filling in along with a temporary dentist who was from Arkansas. He and his wife would stay in a hotel, and he would work for three weeks. Then they would visit family in Arkansas for a week. He wasn't sure if he was returning to our office in August or going to substitute in another state.

He was a really nice fellow Christian, and he had the same name as my deceased brother, Todd. It takes time to develop a flow with new teammates. I usually would be super excited looking forward to Romania but this year I was very weary.

On top of trying to get acclimated to another dental office again, I was taking care of all the last-minute preparations and beginning to pack all the dental supplies for our mission trip. I was also preparing my sermon for the first Sunday we would be in Romania. I was asked to share the message at a church in Jina, Romania. Matthew 5:15 says, "Neither do people light a lamp and put it under a bowl. Instead, they put it on its stand, and it gives light to everyone in the house. In the same way let your light shine before others, that they may see your good deeds and glorify your Father in heaven."

My message was that during the storms of this world our human tendency is to isolate, coverup, or withdraw during the storm. Each of these reactions are like putting a bowl over our light. When we continue to serve others and use the gifts God has given us to encourage those around us, our lights are actually magnified during the storm instead of covered up.

July was a typical Beth and Rod month. Beth hosted a huge Fourth of July gathering at our home for family and friends. We were blessed with the news that our youngest daughter who had lost a baby and had cancer two years ago was expecting our eleventh grandchild in January. The weekend before we would leave on our mission trip to Romania, I helped Beth host our ninth annual pig roast for over one hundred people. Every year I slept outside in a tent with our grandchildren. We needed a new and bigger tent this year because six of my dear babies were snuggled in the tent this year.

The day after the pig roast we hosted a birthday party for our daughter Kari and her husband Zach's three kids—Lexi, ten, Liam, five, and Landry, three. What fun when you have a birthday party on a lake with watersports and bonfires. The next evening Beth hosted her monthly Young Mom's Night Out dinner. Beth was just beaming as she prepared for and then hosted the evening. There aren't many people that would host three gatherings on three consecutive days that were 25–100 people in size! My terminal cancer wife with the gift of hospitality reveled in serving others and God multiplied it back to her manyfold. Days later we were on the plane for Romania!

REFUGE REFLECTIONS

1. Do you ever get frustrated when things don't go the way you expected? I thought I took a job fifteen minutes from home, yet I found myself instead working in two different offices that were an hour from my home.

2. We often see storms as roadblocks or detours to our plans! Are you frustrated that things aren't working out the way you planned?

3. During the season of Lent, as I focused on the sinless Son of God being falsely accused and being tortured and crucified, I began to realize what it meant to "take up your cross and follow him." I began to see that trusting God in the detours and roadblocks was really a form of taking up my cross and following him.

4. When I let go and let God, I began to see the storm's detours as opportunities. I would have never intentionally worked in those two offices. When I let go of my plans, I began to see God's opportunities! In what area of your life do you need to let go of your plans so you can see God's opportunities?

5. How could God be using the detours and roadblocks of your life storms? Are you in places where God hopes to grow you and in contact with people that God intends for you to serve?

CHAPTER 15
Slammed from Every Side

God was using Beth and my life together to write the sermon on letting your light shine, even in the storms of life for the first Sunday we were in Romania. As we drew closer to leaving for Romania, Beth began a cough. Often, she took cough medicine and in a few days, it cleared up. The day before we were to leave for Romania, I took Beth to the doctor and she was placed on an antibiotic. We had started to go on five-mile bike rides again. Apparently, the rides were too much for Beth's knee and it began to ache. My sweetheart was coughing and limping as we boarded the plan for Romania.

All went well with our flight to Romania and after a three-hour bus ride we arrived in Sibui at close to 11:00 p.m. Romanian time, which is 7:00 a.m. Michigan time. We were so tired, and Beth was really coughing. We would be spending the first few days with a Romanian pastor and his wife and daughter. Morning came quickly and I was humbled to preach the sermon in church about being a "light in the darkness of the storms of life" at Pastor Dan's church.

How did a country boy from Michigan get to Eastern Europe for the sixth time with the privilege of sharing the gospel? It is all in God's time and in his power! My quiet, behind the scenes Beth actually stood up and gave about a three-minute testimonial. I had been telling her she had been given a platform with this cancer journey and she needed to share how God was strengthening and using us. My mild-mannered wife stood up and shared her story!

Not only did we have six new people from our church on the team this year, but my sister Vicki was returning for the second time and her daughter Kaylee, a nurse was on our team. Our dear daughter Kristi was on the team for the third year in a row.

Beth and Kristi were again the smiling faces of our mission team doing triage. They would take health histories and blood pressures and determine the needs of the patients! I loved to take breaks and just watch my sweet girls sharing the love of Jesus!

The first day was always the day when new teammates and translators met and jelled. This year, for some reason, we were short on translators the first day. Two of my sisters in Christ from our church were doing the children's ministry and they did not have a translator in the morning. It is really hard to relate with children when you can't speak the language.

I was kind of frustrated because I had recruited them. They had spent a lot of money to be in Romania and were really limited without a translator. I boldly gave them my translator from the dental office for the afternoon. I had been taking an online class to learn Romanian. God provided for me! I knew the Romanian words for: "I am the dentist, where is your problem, open, close, pressure, pain." The other dentist across the room was Romanian and could help with my communications!

On my five previous trips to Romania, we were never short on translators. I planned to really speak up at our team meeting and devotion that night after dinner. As the day went on, I got wearier in the dental clinic and more frustrated inside. Our leader, Steve, at our team meeting asked if anyone had anything they wanted to share. I sure did!

Instead of calling on me, he called on a team member Dora, who was a pharmacist from Atlanta. Dora said, "Could we start with someone sharing a win from today?" Many people were sharing wins! In spite of the translator shortage God had done unbelievable things in our first day. It is quite amazing how if we focus on our blessings, our difficulties and challenges tend to pale in comparison. Needless to say, I didn't voice my concerns and the rest of the week the Lord provided additional translators!

Each day Beth's cough slowly seemed to improve. We also realized, despite Beth's cough and limp, that we had been placed in the home of Pastor Dan and Anna as a listening ear, and as encouragers. They were going through a difficult season of ministry. We were the perfect married couple to be there for them. During our time in full-time ministry, we had experienced similar attacks by Satan and false accusations by church members. Every year we stayed in a hotel. This year we spent four nights in the homes of Romanian church members and the rest of the ten days in a hotel. God knew Dan, Anna, Beth, and I were to connect.

Every morning at the hotel, I would start the day with the Lord just like I did at home. I would get up at 5:00 a.m. and spend a couple of hours in God's Word, praying, and journaling. So as not to wake Beth up, I would go down by the hotel front desk until 7:00 a.m. when I would go to the room and wake up Beth.

Over the years in Romania, I was able to subtly connect spiritually with the person working at the front desk. I was looking and ready for openings and God always provided opportunities. Again, our weekly "joining Jesus on his mission" small group made us realize anywhere and at any time, God may want to use us to extend his Kingdom.

We did not have as much dental help as some years and I definitely felt the weariest of any trip I had ever been on. Something was missing from our experience this year. I couldn't put my finger on it. Satan was definitely stirring things up as he is so good at doing. I also noticed that one of our members, James, who I had met on our first trip, seemed quiet all week. I had definitely wanted to connect with James in the months ahead to get his impressions as we prepared for Romania 2019.

As weary and challenged as Beth and I felt physically, nothing prepared us for the facetime call with our daughter Kari and her husband Zach while we were on the trip. We knew Zach, who was head of IT for a firm, was unhappy with his job and was looking for another job. They informed us they were moving to Grand Rapids about a month after we would return from Romania.

The news of them moving hit really hard! We had moved to Marshall nine years before when their oldest, Lexi, was less than a year old. Beth had lovingly watched their three children one or two days a week when Kari worked as a dental hygienist. With us living on a lake, Kari and the kids were always at our home. Their presence was one of the big blessings that took our focus off the storm of Beth's terminal cancer!

How different Beth and my four year TSW/cancer journey would have been without the nearness of Kari, Zach, and kids. Our son Rod and his family had moved in May after two and a half years living with us during the storm and now Kari, Zach, and kids. The one blessing was that they were moving only a little over an hour away and until they bought a house, they would be living next door to our youngest daughter Kristi and her husband Jon and three kids.

The last few days of our mission trip was full of mixed emotions. Because of Beth's cancer we had decided to take a side trip on the way home. In 2017 we had visited Germany. This year, Beth and I, along with our daughter Kristi, my sister Vicki, and niece Kaylee were going to Paris.

I cannot put into words how special it was to see Paris with my sweetheart Beth. We took a bus tour of Paris one day. We toured Notre Dame. Who would have ever guessed this historic cathedral would catch on fire the next year? We were amazed with the size of the Louvre. We saw the Mona Lisa, this country boy!

Our most incredible memory was when we reached the Arc de Triomphe. Because of Beth's knee we asked to use the elevator. It was getting dark when we entered the elevator. As we got to the top of the Arc, we looked across the skyline of Paris just as they lit up the Eiffel Tower. Wow! This Paris experience was most definitely one of the most intimate and romantic moments of our thirty-nine years of marriage.

So often people are moving at such a pace in life that they don't take time for reflection. My daily journaling for the last five years had really helped me to reflect and to really slow down and wait on the Lord to see through his eyes. I have always come back from Romania more appreciative of the blessings in my life. Six trips to Romania had helped me realize, "less is more." Less busyness, less stuff, and more time with the Lord and loved ones. God has shown me as I have slowed down, I have more and more seen the God moments and opportunities that have probably always been there. I had just been moving way too fast to see them.

As we returned to Michigan at the beginning of August, I was returning to the second temporary dentist position that also was an hour's distance from our home. Instead of focusing on the long drive where I was away from my sweetheart, I decided to focus on how God could use me to be a blessing to my patients and my fellow staff members.

Beth was coming up on a year of being in remission with her cancer. For the last nine years we had closely shared our lives with Kari, Zach, and our beautiful grandchildren. Within a month they would be moving to Grand Rapids. Every moment of the next few weeks would be precious.

For the first two weeks after returning from Romania, we were working at a very busy pace in the dental office, but we had a second dentist and some very talented expanded function dental assistants. The staff went out of their way to tell me how much they appreciated me and my caring heart. After the last year it was so nice to have a semblance of consistency and encouragement in my job.

Beth and my time with the Lord was key to helping us focus on all the blessing of our nine years near Kari and Zach and also that God had new and exciting plans for our family in the days ahead. Beth and I were beginning to ask God if we should sell the camp and possibly also move to Grand Rapids. I didn't have a permanent job and Grand Rapids was a large city where there would be many job opportunities and we would be near both our daughter's families.

The semblance of peace in my job only lasted for a couple of weeks. During the last two weeks of August, two dental assistants gave their job notice. The other dentist indicated he would be leaving in September. I was thinking maybe I should start sending out résumés. Did God want me working in a stressful environment while traveling to work over two hours every day? This was precious time I could be spending with my honey girl.

The sudden storms of Kari and Zach moving, along with the continuous battering winds of my job, were nothing compared to the thunderous news we received when Beth went in for her three-month cancer appointment at the end of August with our local oncologist, Dr. Shen. We were informed that Beth's cancer was back!

I looked back at my daily journal entry the morning after we got the news about Beth's cancer. I wrote the words of John 9:3. This verse had become our life verse as a couple. "This happened so that the works of God could be displayed through him (us)!" We had been taking those words to heart for over two years. I wrote a request in my journal that the Lord would never let us lose our focus on the cross! Then I wrote, "We will glorify you with all our strength, now is the time, now is the time, now is the time!"

In the weeks between when we arrived home from Romania and were shocked to hear the news about Beth's cancer, a new song was released as we listened to our local Christian radio station. One day I was driving home from work and I heard the song. I began to tell Beth and she said she had been listening to the radio and she was going to tell me about the song. The song was "Only Jesus" by you guessed it, Casting Crowns! The refrain of Only Jesus says:

"And I, don't want to leave a legacy, I don't care if they remember me, Only Jesus, And I, I've only got one life to live, I'll let every second point to Him, Only Jesus"

At the time we didn't know that like John 9:3 had become our life verse, "Only Jesus" by Casting Crowns would become our life song!

So many people when things are going smooth in their lives tend to slack off on spending time with the Lord in his Word and prayer. Others, when they are going through the storms of life, become depressed and angry with God and also seem to forget about him. Beth and I had come to realize that the squalls of life can come up without warning and that is when our spiritual tank needs to be full. The last few years we both had discovered that listening to contemporary Christian music was so vital to keeping our tanks spiritually full. Beth had Christian music playing all day at home. When I was spending so much time driving to work and back, I was listening to the contemporary Christian music stations.

When "Only Jesus" by Casting Crowns came out, we realized for the first time that the three songs that had profoundly ministered to us over the last four years were all written by Casting Crowns. In the depths of Beth's TSW, where night after night the itching and insomnia were almost overwhelming, the words of "Just Be Held" by Casting Crowns were indelibly written in the depth of our souls. Virtually every word of this song ministered to us and still does.

"Hold it all together, Everybody needs you strong, But life hits you out of nowhere, And barely leaves you holding on, So when you're on your knees and answers seem so far away, You're not alone, stop holding on and just be held, Your world's not falling apart, it's falling into place, I'm on the throne, stop holding on and just be held"

Just be held! Lie in the arms of the Lord trusting him. Just hold Beth! There was nothing I could say. Beth just needed to know that I was always there for her, just like the Lord was always there for us! Our trust and strength were all in the cross of Jesus Christ.

One year into Beth's cancer, we took a leap of faith and bought the camp. When we were rushing to roof the camp building before leaving for Romania an intense storm blew up and I knew it was obvious the plaster ceiling was destroyed in the area that was not completely roofed. I went outside, raised my hands and sang the song, "Praise You in This Storm" by Casting Crowns. The words of this song so ministered to us.

As we were processing the blowing in of multiple storms, the words of those three songs by Casting Crowns, along with God's Word, gave us the strength and hope only God could provide. My journal two days after we got the news of Beth's cancer showed how powerfully God's Word could be for us, his children. The passage 2 Corinthians 4:8–9 says, "We are hard pressed on every side, but not crushed, perplexed but not despaired, persecuted but not abandoned, struck down, but not destroyed!"

As I was writing this book our country was experiencing the COVID-19 pandemic. During this time, I had tried to seek good information through the media and social media. I, as many others, were experiencing more fear, division, and hopelessness than at any point in our lives.

I actually had taken a break from writing this book due to personally feeling quite sad for my country and the future of my children and grandchildren. I then realized that what Beth and I discovered and experienced during our TSW/cancer journey was exactly what the people of our country and the world needed to hear about and discover.

The secret God had taught Beth and I over the last four years was that the only way to experience peace in the storm was to keep our eyes on the cross of Jesus! I know that is such a cliché, but so often in life we live as though we are running the show. We acknowledge there is a God. We even may belong to a church, regularly worship, and may even volunteer. But we tend to feel like we are in charge and when the storms of life kick up, then we will say, Help God!

As I reflected, it was the multiple storms of life that led Beth and me to trust God and look to him for direction, strength, joy, and hope. We had three converging storms crashing and raining down on us and yet we did not feel the fear and hopelessness our country was experiencing at the time of this writing. Beth's cancer was back, storm one. How was the long drive to my stressful job, storm two, going to impact my ability to care for Beth? This cancer treatment would be much lonelier with Rod and Danielle and kids no longer living with us! Kari and Zach and family would be moved do Grand Rapids by the time Beth's treatment would restart. Storm three, support of family wouldn't be close!

Then there was that leap of faith, the camp which we purchased a little over a year previously. Do we sell the camp or continue to invest money in a dream, all while being buffeted on all sides by the storms of life? As humans and as a married couple, it was so natural to become overwhelmed, depressed to the point of getting a brain ache. We had that need to be in control and to somehow know the future.

Beth's cancer was the storm of first priority. After a number of tests and consultations, a course of treatment was determined. About a week after her first IV chemo day, Beth shared with me she was scared and hurting! Beth never complained. When she said she was hurting it had to be really bad. A few times I could tell because the light in her beautiful green eyes would be dim. We had been praying for a miracle every day, not focusing on the "what ifs" of the future. Living everyday focusing on using our gifts in the present to encourage and bring hope to others. But the cancer was back!

Beth wanted to start making videos for all our children and grandchildren's future big life events. She didn't want them to forget her. When she was diagnosed, they said there was no cure. She was given 18–24 months. We were also told if she went into remission, every future remission would be shorter. Her first remission was about a year. Beth didn't say it but she, for the first time, was coming to grips with the fact she was dying.

I told her that day, "When you start preparing to die, you will quit living!" We decided to live out the words of the latest Casting Crowns song. "Only Jesus" gave us a point of focus, purpose, and peace … "I don't want to leave a legacy, I don't care if they remember me, Only Jesus, I've only got one life to live, I'll let every second point to him, Only Jesus" We didn't realize it that day, but our conversation and the words of that song truly determined our life choices and how we would get up and live each day in the year ahead!

How could I be there for Beth in her cancer journey with my job situation. We lost two staff members in August, which definitely made it much more stressful with our patient load. In September another staff person left and one was fired. On top of that the other dentist decided to move back to Arkansas. As much as I was so blessed to care for my patients and to encourage others faith walk, I was driving an hour each way and was beat tired when I got home.

Instead of giving my notice, I asked the head of Human Resources if I could go down to part time and pay for part of my health insurance benefits. The answer was a resounding, no! With Beth's treatment I wanted to keep our insurance to the end of the year. There was no way I could survive that long and be the husband Beth needed.

Toward the end of October, I took a day and prayed and fasted. It was evident I was supposed to give my six-week notice. I would be done on December 6. My insurance would extend to the end of the year. Knowing there was an end to the way too busy schedule and travel really helped me focus on the blessing of serving the patients and not the very weary schedule.

Even though our children were no longer in Marshall, Kristi blessed us with many trips to Marshall to spend the chemotherapy day with her mom. She often brought us a meal (definitely picked that up from her mom). In addition, we would make regular weekend trips to Grand Rapids and would switch off staying with our daughter's families. Also, when we were in Grand Rapids, we were now only an hour away from our son Rod and his wife Danielle and kids. I guess God knew we needed the support of our loving family, but he also wanted us to get out of the house and out of town. God was blessing us mightily in a different way, through our family. By us traveling more we would come in contact with many new people that God would use us to bless!

The big decision in the midst of the converging storms was, "What to do with the camp." We had almost totally renovated the camp building. It had been a real family affair restoring the building built in the 1950s. When we bought the camp, I felt God wanted to use it to encourage families and children. Since the day we bought the camp, I sensed our children and grandchildren, who used to live in Marshall, would be part of the plan. Now what?

When we found out Beth's cancer was back and that Kari and Zach were moving, I called a realtor to put the camp up for sale. We were to meet with him the next day to sign papers. One thing we learned during the cancer journey was to not make decisions when emotions were high. Rather, be patient, seek counsel. and pray. I spoke with my son Rod who had helped restore the camp building. He questioned if we should put the camp up for sale. Beth and I spent much time in prayer that night.

The next morning, I called the realtor and canceled the appointment. When you take up your cross and follow him, it gives you courage! Our prayer time led us to feel God didn't want us to sell the camp. He wanted us to trust and instead make a big financial investment of flooring, heating and air conditioning, and kitchen cabinets.

In the words of my middle son, Reid, this "wasn't our first rodeo" when it came to cancer treatment. We were prepared for sleepless nights, bone pain, upper respiratory infections. Over the next few months, we experienced them all. But Beth and I were in the storm together. I just cuddled Beth and whispered, "We are perfect puzzle pieces!"

REFUGE REFLECTIONS

1. As you look back on your life, are there seasons where Satan saw a storm in your life as an opportunity to detour you? Satan does his best work when he has us isolated in a storm of life.

2. Satan is the master of getting people to make snap decisions in the storms of life. We almost put the camp up for sale. Why didn't Satan win this time? Beth and I prayed and sought counsel from our son. Is there an area Satan is tempting you to make a snap decision? Are you praying? Who can you seek good counsel from?

3. My year-long job situation was one of the more interesting times of my professional career. I could have become so consumed with the long-distance travel or the ever-changing staff situations. In the end it turned out to be a time of personal growth for me. Much prayer, patience, and counsel allowed this season to ultimately be a blessing. Are you in a season where you feel like God has forgotten about you? He hasn't! Hold onto the words of Romans 8:28, "And we know that in all things God works for the good of those who love Him, who have been called according to His purpose."

CHAPTER 16

Keep Your Eyes on the Lighthouse

Beth began chemo shortly after Labor Day. I truly believe when people have no purpose they despair and are consumed with fear. "Only Jesus" was and would always be our purpose! Beth was in her element cooking and entertaining. When the storms of life hit many people throw a pity party! My sweetheart with the love language of service and the gift of hospitality threw people parties!

Those words of the song "Just Be Held" by Casting Crowns are so true, "When your eyes are on the storm, You wonder if I love you still, But if your eyes are on the cross, You know I always have and always will"

We had discovered so many blessings in the storm! Beth was in her element with her eye on the cross when she was entertaining. The cross was truly our lighthouse leading us through the storm. Most people had no idea how many sleepless nights we experienced along with the bone pain, upper respiratory infections, and urinary tract infections that were just a part of Beth's life. The reason they didn't know is because of the strength and encouragement she received as she lived every second for Jesus.

Beth looked forward with excitement to hosting the monthly dinner for the young moms. That was always a high point for both of us. Most of our children were not living in town now, but it seemed like most weekends one of the families were visiting for the weekend. The other weekends we were visiting them.

It felt so good to be used by God to bless others. Beth was again the organizer for our church Thanksgiving dinner. Each year on the day of the church Thanksgiving service, members of the church would set up all the table and chairs after our second worship service. Beth and I would then have the afternoon alone together to set up all the food tables and decorate the tables. Beth's green eyes just glowed with excitement as she would each year decorate in a different creative way that was all Beth!

So many people dread the time it takes to shop for Christmas gifts. Beth was in her element shopping and wrapping gifts for the soon to be eleven grandchildren along with our five married children and spouses. This year was no different! There was never stress, just joy, connected with this process.

Beth was very much a tradition person. She had many traditions our children and now grandchildren had come to enjoy and expect. Beth took each granddaughter when they were six years old on a train trip to Chicago to buy an American Girl doll.

When Beth's cancer returned, I know she was wondering how much time she had. She spent much time sewing handmade nightgowns for each granddaughter and their American Girl doll. She also sewed matching aprons and baker's hats for the granddaughters and their American Girl dolls. She sewed many extra sets for future granddaughters.

In addition to this, she also sewed aprons for my two daughters and three daughters-in-law for Christmas. Needless to say, Beth stayed busy between hosting events, chemo treatment, Christmas shopping, and sewing until I quit my job in December. She was so excited, as always. Those beautiful green eyes just lit up when she was entertaining or shopping and sewing for others.

Beth and I were so blessed when the youth of our church used the camp for a weekend in early November. Beth also hosted her Young Moms November Thanksgiving gathering at the Camp.

Every other year our entire Knoerr clan celebrated Thanksgiving together. On the off year our children gathered with their in-laws. This was our year. The warm glow of the two wood fireplaces at the camp couldn't compare to the warmth our hearts felt as we gathered with our beautiful family, twenty-two, almost twenty-three of us!

The day after Thanksgiving it was our tradition to go with our daughter Kari's family to a tree farm to see Santa and get our Christmas trees. Also, on the Friday after Christmas Beth always had over a hundred cutout Christmas cookies baked that needed to be frosted. From a very young age our children and now grandchildren helped frost the cookies. Usually, by Sunday night of Thanksgiving weekend, Beth would have our house decorated like a Christmas wonderland.

As I sat on our couch with my adorable wife, again taking in the most beautifully decorated home imaginable, we were looking ahead to May when we would celebrate forty years of marriage. We were, for the first time in our marriage, wearing matching flannel pajamas, courtesy of my sweet honey girl. The coming Advent season drew our focus to the birth of the Christ child who would one day sacrifice his life for all mankind. Beth loved serving her Lord and her family during this season.

For almost two years we had hosted a small group in our home on Thursdays. When Beth's cancer came back, we discontinued the group in September. Beth wanted to host a Christmas evening with our dear friends in the Lord. What an unbelievable way to thank our friends for being part of a group that taught us how to join Jesus on his mission in hospitals, doctor's offices and wherever we found ourselves. That group helped us see our purpose amid the storm!

December 6 was my final day at the dental office. I had been driving an hour each way to work for the last seven months. During the six weeks since I gave my notice I had so many opportunities to encourage patients and fellow staff. But now I was entering a new season. I remember waking up the next morning and basically saying, "I am all yours, Lord!" I really wanted to take extra time each day to seek the Lord's plan. I did know that I would have much more time to serve my honey!

Now that I wasn't working in the dental office, I could again spend all day with Beth on her chemotherapy days. As was our routine, we took our Bibles and did our devotion time at the cancer center. We always ended up in great spiritual conversations with the staff. In December we also went on short overnight trips to all five of our children, reveling in the blessings of our family.

We both volunteered at our monthly LIGHTHOUSE food bank at our church. We were part of an overwhelming fifty volunteers who helped with this ministry. I would carry food to people's cars and then get the opportunity to share Jesus's love and pray with them. A week before Christmas I took my sweetheart out to her favorite German restaurant, Zehnders in Frankenmuth, to celebrate her birthday a few days early.

After dinner, God kept nudging me to drive an hour and a half out of the way to go to Mott's Children's Hospital at the University of Michigan in Ann Arbor. A young couple who just started worshipping at our church had their first newborn son. He was in need of surgery. We went to the hospital and prayed with the young man who we had just met. He was so blessed!

Over the last four years of TSW/cancer I found myself doing more and more assisting Beth as she lived out her love language of service and the gift of hospitality. I was changing! My joy was now serving the Lord as I assisted Beth in serving and hosting others.

Days before Christmas, Beth and I owned some income rental property and I was showing one of our apartments to a prospective tenant, who was a single mom. I did share my faith with her and mentioned the strength Beth and I were receiving from our faith during her cancer. She informed me that her aunt, her mom's sister, was just diagnosed with stage 4 cancer.

I told her to give her mom our phone number. We would definitely be open to talk with her. Little did I know that the tenant's mom would indeed call us! I boldly offered for Beth and I to come to their house and meet with her and her husband. We ended up sharing our cancer story and how God was our hope and strength. Beth and I prayed with them and we were able to encourage them in the months that followed.

We had no clue how we would look back on this unbelievable Christmas Eve Day with our large family of twenty-two at the camp building. The year before, our first family Christmas gathering at the camp was quite chilly with portable heat. This year the heating system was in place and working great. I can't put into words how blessed we were. Our hearts were filled with gratitude for all the blessings God had showered upon us through our ever-growing family.

One of Beth's Christmas traditions was to sing happy birthday to Jesus with a cake for him. Our oldest grandchildren were now becoming the readers of Luke chapter 2. Beth added a new tradition in 2018 of making costumes for a live Nativity Scene with our grandchildren. One-year-old Hank was baby Jesus. We capped off our day by all being in church for the Christmas Eve evening worship service!

As special as Christmas Eve was for Beth and me, what really stood out as I look at that month of December was the way in which we focused on our blessings and serving others, instead of the storm of terminal cancer. I jotted a quote in my journal in early December that summed up how God had helped us discover how to live life, "Surrender is experiencing the joy of watching God's plan unfold!"

The day after Christmas in my prayers God said, "Go on an appreciate aunts and uncles tour!" Over a two-day period, we were able to visit and personally thank many of our aunts and uncles for the part they had played in our lives!

At the beginning of 2018 Beth had committed to journal each day. When the cancer storm swept back in August, she quit journaling. Beth did have two entries at the end of November. In her one entry she was imploring the Lord for a miracle of healing! "I really need a miracle!" The second entry was all gratitude on

Thanksgiving Day 2018. She thanked the Lord for our children and grandchildren. She said "Thank you for the cross and resurrection and what it gives me ... eternal life." Then she wrote, "I love my babies so much and I want them to BE THERE." I never ever remembered Beth using the phrase BE THERE, meaning that they would all know the Lord and be there in heaven someday. Beth would use this phrase again in the months ahead.

On New Year's Eve we reflected on the year 2018 and looked ahead to 2019. Beth and I both looked to the next year as God's year, a time for us to extend a spiritual legacy (Only Jesus). Little did we know what that meant!

REFUGE REFLECTIONS

1. Have you ever been in a time of your life where you couldn't see "up from down?" Are you having a difficult time prioritizing right now? Keep your eyes on the Lighthouse!

2. We were slammed with two tidal waves, Beth's cancer was back and Kari and Zach and family were moving out of town. Life was already pretty choppy with my interesting dental office situation. Casting Crowns helped us "Keep the Main Thing the Main Thing." Only Jesus!

3. Have you lost track of the main thing? The words of Casting Crowns will get you back on track and keep you on track, "I don't want to leave a legacy, Only Jesus, I only have one life to live, let every second point to him, Only Jesus!"

4. Look at every area of your life and ask yourself, "How can I let every second point to him, Only Jesus?"

CHAPTER 17

Blindsided by the Tidal Wave

As we moved into 2019, I couldn't help but reflect on the verse from Proverbs 31:10, "A wife of noble character who can find? She is worth more than rubies!" As we started the new year it had been almost a month since I had quit making the long drive back and forth to the dental office. As I reflected on the last almost five-year TSW/cancer journey, I couldn't help but praise and thank the Lord with every fiber of my being for my amazing, amazing wife!

In a little over four months, we would celebrate our fortieth wedding anniversary. We decided to go on a ten-day Caribbean cruise to celebrate our forty years of marriage. We went on our first cruise in 2017, just before Beth's inpatient chemotherapy. When your wife is given 18–24 months to live, you go! We had hoped to take all five of our children and spouses on a cruise, but with Beth's cancer back there wasn't time to make it happen so we went together.

Two days before we were to leave on January 6, Beth was scheduled for her IV chemo. Her immunities were too low, she couldn't have the chemo treatment. Dr. Shen told us that Beth's blood numbers indicated she was in clinical remission. When he left the room, Beth teared up and said the weirdest thing to me given the supposedly good news. She said, "What if I don't have much time?"

I took a moment to collect myself. Then I gently replied to my sweet honey, Beth, "Then we will squeeze life out of every day!"

We were sitting at the airport in Detroit waiting to board our flight. Out of the blue I received an email advertising an online mentoring opportunity for new authors by Jack Canfield, the author of the "Chicken Soup for the Soul" books, called "Best Seller Blueprint." I showed Beth and quickly put a big hit on my credit card before jumping on our flight. I had been playing with the idea of writing a book to share what God had been showing Beth and I over the last over four years of TSW/cancer treatment. The title that was on my heart that day was "Don't Waste This Storm."

This cruise was a gift from God. The health challenges of the last few years had drawn Beth and I very close, yet this ten-day cruise was a time of ultimate relaxation, reflection, and renewal with my sweetheart.

When I was a young dentist, an older patient once told me that going on a week vacation was a waste. I asked him what he meant. He told me that in a week vacation you spend the first half of the week de-stressing from work and the last half of the week stressing as you prepared to go back to work. His theory was that you never really slow down and relax!

Our first five-day Caribbean cruise two years prior was awesome, but I do think we were looking ahead to the coming chemo and didn't truly slow down mentally and just relax. Through much of our married life together this would happen with our daily and weekly time with the Lord. The busyness of family, jobs, and even church activities often squeezed out the most important time of rest and relaxation with the Lord.

Over the last few years, God was breaking and changing us. Time with him and each other each morning was now a nonnegotiable time each day. I encouraged my married children to set aside regular time together as couples apart from their children.

While on this cruise we truly lived out the words of Casting Crowns in "Just Be Held." We laid in the arms of each other and the Lord and were overwhelmed with the beauty of the Caribbean, the blessings of our marriage, family, and all God had blessed us with.

Our focus on the cross of Jesus and our blessings kept us from being worried and overwhelmed with the challenges and uncertainties of Beth's cancer!

When Beth and I came to this realization in our walk of faith, all we could think of was sharing this with others! We had so many opportunities to share our faith with cruise staff, tour guides, and many of our fellow passengers. As we jumped on the plane back to Michigan we were overflowing with gratitude and love for all God had blessed us with.

We came home rested and energized. We were ready to discover God's plan to use us! We were told Beth could not have knee replacement surgery because her immunities were too low. We planned to ask the orthopedic surgeon to consider replacing Beth's knee in spite of her low immunities. We had things to do and people to serve!

Beth and I came back to our beautiful family and our busy life. We were welcomed back home from the cruise by most of our large family at the birthday party for two of our grandchildren, Calvin and his sister Charleigh. Within a couple of weeks, Calvin, Charleigh, and their brother Caleb would be welcoming grandbaby number eleven into our beautiful family!

The next evening Beth hosted fifteen young moms including our daughters Kristi and Kari for the monthly Young Moms Night Out dinner. This would be the second year that Beth would provide small canvases and all the moms painted their word for the year. Last year Beth's one word for the year was JOY. Her one word for 2019 was HOPE. Beth's favorite verse was Jeremiah 29:11, "I know the plans I have for you declares the Lord. Plans to prosper you and not to harm you. Plans to give you HOPE and a future!" This evening continued the excitement and hope that we brought back with us from the cruise!

The next morning, we were up early. Beth had to have a number of blood tests and then we would meet with Dr Shen a few hours later, with her IV chemo treatment to follow. Beth's platelets had been quite low the day after we got back from the cruise, so we expected she would not be getting her IV chemo. We were sitting in Dr. Shen's office waiting for him. He came in a few minutes later and sat down at his desk and with no warning or preparation said, "Have you thought about hospice? With your blood test numbers you fit in the realm of three months to live!"

It was like we were hit by a tidal wave. I had never experienced such a moment. Over the last few years, I really felt like I was letting go and letting God. But as a human we are all trying to paddle on our own to stay afloat in the storms of life. For the first time in my life, I had nothing! I was totally resting in the Lord's life preserver of faith! It was keeping my honey and I afloat!

Dr. Shen wanted us to be seen at the University of Michigan

and get a bone marrow biopsy to better assess Beth's cancer! As Beth was receiving IV immunoglobulins all afternoon to increase her platelet numbers, I went out into the hallway and called all five of our children. It was the hardest, most difficult conversations I had ever had with each of them. My babies were so emotional. I think for the first time we were all facing the fact that Beth may not beat the cancer and her time with us on earth may be short!

God knew way back in October that I should not be working and available to support Beth. I cannot imagine if I had been working and my sweet baby girl had received that news from Dr. Shen by herself. I couldn't help but remember the surprising words of Beth from her last doctor's appointment before the cruise, "What if I don't have much time?" Beth somehow deep inside knew!

We had to wait until the next Monday, six whole days until we would see Dr. Ye at the University of Michigan Cancer Center. We had no clue what tomorrow would bring, but we would be resting in God's arms and each other's! We would continue to live out the words of John 9:3, "This happened so that the works of God could be displayed through (us)!"

Monday finally arrived! We went to Ann Arbor and Beth had more blood tests and her bone marrow biopsy. Dr Ye felt if Beth's white blood cell count increased, she could be accepted into a study with a promising new treatment! It would take about five weeks for all the results to come back.

We drove home with renewed hope for a possible new treatment. Over the last almost three years we lived life with the attitude, "stay in the game hopefully until there is a game changer!" We were hoping this new experimental treatment would be the "game changer."

A few days later we were looking to the next day, because it would be our sweet Kristi's birthday. She had shared the topical steroid journey with Beth and then also beat cancer two years ago. We went to bed thanking God for our beautiful daughter and for the soon to be eleventh grandbaby that she was due to deliver any day! We were also prayerfully preparing for the next morning when a film crew would be coming to film Beth and I for a promotional video for our local hospital oncology clinic.

Beth and I took the opportunity to share about our journey and our faith with the marketing company owner and those setting up to film. We shared our Bible verse John 9:3 and how we saw each day and each hospital visit as an opportunity to share the source of our hope!

Beth and I told them how we had gone on three mission trips to Romania trusting God, even though, due to chemo, Beth had low immunities and was encouraged by her oncologist not to go. We shared with them that she recently was given three months to live. They were incredulous that we were still planning on going to Romania in July.

Beth shared in the filming that having a local cancer center in Marshall allowed us to lead a fairly normal life spending time with our children, grandchildren, and church. She also emphasized how the staff at the center were like friends. We knew about their families, and they knew about ours. To sum it up, we lived each day to the fullest.

I ended our portion of the filming by sharing how we started every day. For over four years I would start every day by asking Beth, "What's today?"

She would then answer, "The day you love me more than yesterday."

Then I shared how we ended each day when I would ask her, "What's tomorrow?"

Beth would answer, "The day you love me more than today!" The best part of the filming was the picture at the end where they captured me hugging Beth with tears of deep love in my eyes!

As we were talking about our faith with the marketing company owner and the film crew, we really didn't know if any of them were followers of Jesus. The owner of the marketing company told us as they were packing up to leave our home, that we didn't need to go on mission trips to Romania because we were on a mission trip every day!

Beth and I did an internal fist pump! Yes, people were seeing that we had "joined Jesus on his mission" in our daily lives. There is nothing better than to be used by the Lord to share the love and hope of Jesus!

Just as the film crew was walking out the door, my phone rang and the area code of the call was Ann Arbor. I knew it was the University of Michigan Cancer Center. It had only been three days since our appointment. Our doctor told us it would take three weeks for the test results.

Sure enough, it was our University of Michigan oncologist. It was not what I wanted to hear. She told me that Beth's bone marrow was 90 percent cancer. Because of such high numbers, Beth would not qualify for the new treatment trials. Beth's oncologist said they needed a "big gun" treatment, but a "big gun" would kill Beth!

Wow! I sat and held my sweetheart as we wept tears that expressed more than any words could have expressed. How would we tell our children? We decided to wait a few weeks so as not to take away from the joy of the baby that was due any day! A few hours later Kristi called us and let us know she was in labor and headed to the hospital. At about 10:00 p.m. that night we saw our beautiful new granddaughter.

Kristi and Beth were so close as mother and daughter. I wanted to tell Kristi about her mom's three-month prognosis so she would maybe use Beth as a middle name to honor my honey's memory. But I didn't want to share such sad new on such a joyous day.

Kristi and Jon gave our sweet granddaughter the name Channdler Marie. Channdler usually is spelled with only one N. But they used two Ns to honor Beth. Beth's middle name is ANN!

February 1 was the epitome of an up and down and up day. Our eyes were focused on the love of God shown us in his Son and shown us in our family that had grown to twenty-three with the addition of baby Channdler and not on the ever-changing and raging storm of cancer! We might be in a storm, but Jesus was in the boat with us!

Beth had a tradition of spending the first week after a baby was born with both our daughters. This would be the first time with me not working. I would be able to be a part of the first week tradition. Channdler came home from the hospital late on Saturday night.

When I got up early for my devotion time and to get ready for church, Beth was already up. This almost never happened. As I entered Kristi and Jon's dining room I took in the most blessed sight. My sweetheart Beth was holding a sleeping baby Channdler, while sitting at the dining room table with her Bible open. This was a perfect picture of my wife and her life priorities … her faith and her family! As I was taking in the sight, Beth quietly said to me, "She won't know me." I told Beth that I would spend the rest of my life telling her about you! If Beth only knew how God would use Channdler in the days ahead!

A few hours later we were in church with both our daughter's families. God painted this unbelievable picture of Beth's name. It truly was a message from God. Beth's "One Word" for the year 2019 was hope. It was like God painted Beth's name in the sky. Beth's name was an acronym for BE The Hope, BETheHope.

My quiet grace filled wife through her gift of hospitality and through simple acts of kindness had throughout her life shown others the hope that is only found in Christ. A few weeks later I showed my daughters my nonartistic creation. By then the "T" of Beth's name had become a cross of Jesus. This logo, Be The Hope most definitely was centered on the cross of Jesus Christ. I began praying and asking God if he had a ministry or nonprofit foundation in mind.

As we began the first week of February after Channdler's birth, the height of the waves in our storm called life could not have been higher. Beth was given months to live by Dr. Shen. The only treatment option he gave us had a prognosis of 50 percent to live a year. He also said Beth would probably spend half the time in the hospital.

Beth and I didn't feel good about the treatment recommendation. God knew way back in October when I gave my six-week notice that we would be hit by a cancer storm for this part of our journey like none we had experienced. I needed to be available 24/7 to walk with, together seek counsel, and above all support my dear honey.

With no sight of shore in the storm and with the waves raging over our head, together we waited on the Lord each morning in prayer and in God's Word. Each Sunday we raised our hands in praise to the one who sacrificed his life for Beth and me. We also learned to allow our brothers and sisters in Christ the privilege of loving on us and praying for us. We had not shared with anyone but our children the original 18–24 months terminal cancer prognosis. As a result, our friends and extended family were in shock.

The women from the Young Mom's group that Beth hosted monthly along with men from our Fight Club ministry had a twenty-four-hour time of prayer for Beth. Every half hour a different person prayed. It was humbling and powerful.

After a few weeks of prayer and discussion, God began to show us the way amid the raging storm and we made an appointment with a naturopathic oncologist. He said he could put Beth on a Mediterranean diet, recommended daily exercise and told us he could not cure her but could aid in the process and reduce the side effects of chemo. He recommended we get more than one second opinion.

A week later we drove to Grand Rapids near our daughters' homes to see a traditional oncologist. Instantly we felt like he was an answer from God. He definitely did not like the treatment option we had been given. He said his role was to prolong Beth's life, not end it! We did not seek another opinion in Chicago where many had encouraged us to go. We felt treatment in Michigan would allow us to continue to lead as normal of a life as possible near our dear family.

The plan was to start chemotherapy the following Wednesday, which just happened to be Ash Wednesday. As we were journeying into a season of chemotherapy, we were also entering Lent and were following the journey of our Savior Jesus to the cross. Each three-week chemotherapy cycle would have daily oral chemo along with one day of IV chemotherapy each week.

Just because we began to see a path through the storm didn't mean it would be smooth. Over the next two months, Beth would experience severe bone and back pain. After the first week of IV chemo, Beth ended up in the hospital for three days and did not receive any IV chemo for the rest of the first cycle because her hemoglobin, platelets, and white blood cells that fight infection were too low. The second cycle she did get in almost three full weeks of IV chemo.

The morning of Beth's second cycle last IV chemo she woke up with a fever and rolled her ankle. My battle tested sweetheart limped into the cancer center on crutches. They did indeed still give her the chemo! Praise the Lord! After extreme back pain for a few weeks and multiple trips to the chiropractor, a back radiograph determined the cancer had caused a compression fracture to Beth's T-8 vertebrae. Beth now started wearing a back brace to go along with her knee brace and ankle brace!

REFUGE REFLECTIONS

1. Read and reflect on Mark 4:35–41. Are you astounded by the disciple's lack of trust? Jesus is literally in the boat with them.

2. Are you or do you know someone who is in a life storm where you are wondering if the Lord doesn't care if you drown? Jesus is not only in the boat with you, he is sleeping! Can you truly surrender in the fiercest storms to the one who gave everything for you, even his life?

3. Have you ever experienced the peace of total surrender to the Lord? Jesus words to your present storm is, "Quiet! Be still!" So many times in my life I thought I had surrendered, then I would start trying to paddle. When Beth was given 3 months to live, I believe we came as close as humanly possible to totally surrendering to the one who could calm the storm. Surrender allows us to experience a peace and a purpose in the storm like we could never have imagined.

CHAPTER 18

Go Big or Go Home

God over the last five years had over and over shown us if we looked to him during the storm and were open to opportunities to serve him, the Lord would be faithful and would not leave us or forsake us, but would bless us and encourage us to his glory!

Two weeks after our beautiful Channdler was born, on the same day we found out Beth's bone marrow was 90 percent cancer, a guest pastor spoke at our church and emphasized the verse that had become our life verse, John 9:3, "This happened so that the works of God could be displayed through Him (us). It was like an affirmation from heaven to keep on serving.

Instead of hunkering down and covering up in the storm, we said, "Serve people when the storm is raging the hardest. If we as Christ followers are losing it in the storms of life, why would anyone be interested in a relationship with Jesus. On the other hand, if a Jesus follower shows hope and joy and peace in the storm, people will want to know more about what we have."

Matthew 28:18–20, is known as the Great Commission. Jesus says to his disciples, "All authority in heaven and earth has been given to me. Therefore, go and make disciples of all nations, baptizing them in the name of the Father and of the Son and of the Holy Spirit, and teaching them to obey everything I have commanded you. And surely I am with you always, to the very end of the age."

I see the four P's of a Jesus follower's life in the Great Commission. Our PURPOSE is to make disciples. That is a big job! But the next 2 Ps are what make our purpose possible. Jesus says, "all authority in heaven and earth has been given to me!" As followers of Jesus, we by faith have POWER. Jesus had power to rise from the dead. He especially in the storms of life will give us the power to live out our purpose. But that is not all. The third P is his PRESENCE. Jesus says, "and surely I am with you always to the very end of the age." We are not alone; he is always with us! POWER, PURPOSE, PRESENCE! When we live using our gifts, living out our purpose to make disciples in his PRESENCE, by His POWER the result is a PEACE that passes all understand!

So, with the life storm prognosis of 3 months to live …

1. Beth continued her tradition of spending the first week with our daughter Kristi after Channdler was born. Cooking, cleaning, washing clothes, all this while full of cancer!

2. Beth didn't miss a month hosting Young Mom's Dinners in February, March, and April. In February all the young mom's gave Beth handwritten notes. After they left our home, Beth and I read the notes of encouragement and thanksgiving with tear-filled eyes.

3. I was blessed to be the speaker at two Saturday morning men's breakfasts. And who do you think made the breakfasts? Beth!

4. When we drove to Grand Rapids for our first appointment with Dr. Brinker I said to Beth, "Well, we are off on a mission trip to Grand Rapids." We always took our Bibles to Beth's cancer treatment appointments. We shared our faith and strength in Christ with our nurses and other medical staff. They most definitely were encouraged by our faith. We

also had the opportunity to encourage many fellow patients. Pointing them to the One where we could find true hope and strength.

As I was writing this book, I contacted one of the couples where the husband was fighting the same cancer as Beth. I told them I had been praying for them every day for the last year and for their two miracle granddaughters. When I mentioned their names, they were astonished.

5. We had traveled to Romania on a mission trip three times while Beth had cancer. It was time to book flights. Beth was given three months to live in January and the mission trip was in July. Our daughter Kristi had been to Romania three times but our older daughter Kari never had an interest in going.

As I was looking to the beginning of April, I realized it was the twentieth anniversary of the first two worship services of Fellowship of Faith Church. My family had the privilege of helping start this new mission church. My two daughters were thirteen and fifteen years old at the time. One lead worship on a piano on Good Friday and the other on Easter.

I approached our oldest daughter Kari who never felt lead to go on the mission trip to Romania and I said to her, "Wouldn't it be a cool way to celebrate the privilege we had twenty years ago to start a new church together by going to Romania?"

The next day she said she wanted to go. I quickly contacted our mission team leader Steve and told him all four of us— Beth, Kristi, Kari, and I—wanted to be a part of the mission team. A few weeks later he called and said if something happened with Beth, and we had to cancel the team wasn't big enough this year without us. He wondered if he should cancel the mission team. I told him we would pray about it. Our family decision was that unless Beth was near death, Kristi, Kari, and I were going no matter what! The trip was on!

6. For three years I helped Beth live every day to the fullest, praying for a miracle cure. I was still praying for a cure, but the reality of the fact Beth's time with us may be drawing to a close was much more real now! I never talked to my beautiful children about this, but by their actions I could tell they felt the same way.

A few weeks after Beth was given the three-months-to-live prognosis, our two daughters wanted to quickly arrange a family vacation to Florida at the end of March. Beth's first cycle of chemo was not going well. She had been hospitalized and needed regular blood transfusions. I personally felt Beth wasn't stable enough to go. I left the decision up to Beth. She wholeheartedly wanted us to go. It was an unbelievable week. Relaxing while making so many precious family memories!

It had been a couple of years since we had a family picture of the Knoerr clan. We were now twenty-three in number with baby Channdler. My daughters arranged to have our family picture taken at the camp in May, the week before Mother's Day. Again, I think each one of us inside were for the first time wondering if this would be our last family picture.

We were always a close family, but I could sense everyone was making an extra effort to send their children to our house for 3–5-day vacations. We were sleeping overnight in

Grand Rapids at either of our two daughters who were living next to each other. The grandchildren fought for us to sleep at their side of the duplex, so we switched off every other time. At the time, our six-year-old granddaughter Charleigh always wanted to sleep with Beth and me. She has the most caring heart! She was such a little bed hog, but her love for her grandma and grandpa was so tender and precious.

Focusing on our blessings, gratitude, and service to others was how God helped us not just survive but thrive in the storm. That is the fourth Casting Crowns song "Thrive" that had ministered to us in the storm!

Living in the storm while looking to the Lord was really about trust and leaving the major course adjustments to him. We arrived back from the family trip to Florida and Beth began her second cycle of chemo. The first cycle was eventful to say the least. Yet our new oncologist felt even with the small amount of chemo Beth received the cancer was responding.

The night before Easter I was blessed to watch three generations, Beth, Kristi, and Charleigh prepare for our Easter celebration. I prayed that if this was Beth's last Easter, may many come to church on Easter and grow closer to Christ!

As we woke up to a tremendously joyous family Easter morning, Beth tearfully mumbled to me, "I think I am dying!" We talked and I ask Beth if we should consider selling our house on the lake in Marshall and move to Grand Rapids near the girls.

We had finally finished remodeling our house on the lake. It was the center of activity for our water sports family. Yet as I prayed, I felt it would be such a blessing for Beth to live near her daughters and seven grandchildren. If Beth's time was short, I would sure need the love of our family around me. I patiently prayed and waited on the Lord.

For the previous eight months Kari, Zach, and family had been living in the three-bedroom duplex next to our youngest daughter

Kristi and husband Jon, while they searched for a house to buy. A couple of weeks after Easter they announced they were moving out of the duplex and would be buying a house only a mile away from Kristi and Jon. The duplex would be available for new tenants in the middle of June.

Was this the answer to my prayers? Not every son-in-law wants to live next door to his in-laws. As I went to bed my prayer was, "Lord, if this is your will let Jon or Kristi ask us if we want to rent from them?"

The next day I was going to a coffee shop with Beth and my girls. As I was getting into Kristi's vehicle the first thing out of her mouth was, "Jon wants to know if you would like to move in after Kari and Zach move out?" When Beth and I got home I told her about my prayer. We decided to put our house up for sale and move to Grand Rapids.

The month of May flew by beginning with the family pictures at our camp. Beth completed her second chemo cycle. Her three-month-to-live prognosis would not have gotten us to May. I had been counting down days to May 12, our fortieth anniversary. We made it!

Happily, 2019 was the year that Mothers' Day and our anniversary were on the same day. What a blessed day to celebrate the most grace filled, caring wife, mother, and grandmother a man and family could ever imagine having. The next night Beth and I celebrated our fortieth anniversary quietly without a lot of fanfare.

Beth hosted her last Young Mom's Night Out in May. It was exactly three years since Beth was diagnosed with terminal cancer and was asked to host this monthly dinner gathering. It was a night of mixed emotions for Beth and me. Many months because of her insomnia, I would find Beth up in the middle of the night preparing for the Young Mom's Night. In some of Beth's weariest and most pain-filled times these women gave Beth purpose in the storm.

Using Beth's gift of hospitality each month took her focus off the storm. Beth never once saw this monthly gathering as an obligation or a burden. It was such a blessing to Beth and to me. I couldn't wait each month to see Beth's green eyes light up. As the cancer progressed, I more and more helped my honey with preparation and clean up. I lived to hear our house filled with the joyous fellowship of God doing his work through this evening!

Because we were selling our lake house, we did not put the boat in the lake. Our family Memorial Day weekend usually involved a lot of wakeboarding. Instead, my grandkids spent time fishing. They caught seventy-six bluegills. Grandpa did a lot of fish cleaning! But they were so proud taking their own fish off, baiting their hooks and oh what a fish fry. Beth just reveled in the family moments as I did!

Beth had one more four-week cycle before our mission trip to Romania in July. The cancer seemed to be on the run. We had reason to believe that Beth was headed toward another remission. I hadn't drawn a paycheck in almost 6 months. I became aware of a dentist job opportunity where they needed a full-time dentist. When you don't know how much time you will have with your wife, it was hard to think about working again. After much prayer I agreed to work two days a week while they were looking for a full-time dentist.

After only two weeks, another dentist was in the office and he said he would be working full time. I got a text that night from the office manager that I was not needed. My contract required a thirty-day written notice. I understood that they really needed a full-time dentist. But terminate me immediately without notice and then for cause?

My old self would have shifted into "defend my good name mode." The Rod that God had been breaking after much prayer individually and with my Monday morning Men's breakfast group decided to respond graciously and with thanksgiving. I sent a letter to the husband and wife, owner dentists, wishing them the best, offering a few observations that could improve their office and thanking them for the opportunity to work with their staff and care for their patients.

Many dentists would have instead threatened a lawsuit. Beth's cancer journey had taught us to wait on the Lord and to trust him when the waves seemed to suddenly shift in the storms of life. Many people spend so much time proving they are right that they end up suffering and ultimately losing. My God who knew the future wanted me not working, but instead loving on my beautiful sweetheart!

When the waves of life kick up and seem to be coming from many directions it is easy to cry out like the disciples when they were in the boat with Jesus. All Jesus had to say was, "Be still" and the waves responded.

As Beth and I entered June she was starting her fourth cycle of chemo. We were packing our house on the lake, and I was encouraging Beth to try to downsize. I was trying to get our house ready to list with a realtor. We were only a little over a month away from leaving for Romania. I had a lot of planning because I was in charge of the dental clinic and I was also the spiritual leader of our team!

I celebrated Father's Day with our amazing family and two days later we moved into the duplex next to Kristi and Jon. We left our bedroom staged with furniture in our house that was for sale and slept on a mattress and box spring which was on the floor. This was a little hard for Beth with her bone pain and fractured vertebrae. Hopefully we would get an offer on our house, and we could move the rest of our furniture.

Beth was always big on family traditions throughout our marriage. In unpacking from our move, I came across a journal entitled, "The Great Tent Experience." Back in 1999 when my youngest two sons were age five and ten years old, we purchased a small three-man tent that summer. The boys and I slept in it overnight in the back yard a few times. About September I asked the boys if they thought we could sleep in the tent every month of the year. For ten years we did not miss a month. Through the heat of summer and the frigid cold of winter, we did not miss a month!

What I wrote in the beginning of the journal really summed

up how Beth and I looked at and approached the health challenge journey of the last five years. I wrote, "What started out as a wild idea has turned into a tradition and outlook on life that I pray I never forget. When you are in the tent, there is no material things, just a father and his children and love that fills the tent with a warmth that far surpasses all the things people think are important. When I lie in the tent with my babies, I know I am the most blessed man in the world. To share over twenty-two years of marriage with Beth, five unbelievable children, what more could a man ask for. As we hug and kiss and snuggle in that tent we are brought back to the basics of life, God and family. I thank God for allowing us to stumble on this tradition. I look forward to the times we will share in the years ahead!"

My journal entry in December 2001 was, "I hope someday to continue this tradition with my grandkids!" The grandkids and I had a tradition of sleeping in the tent the night before our annual pig roast. Beth and I decided to restart the monthly tent sleepover tradition. The week before we would leave for Romania, I slept in the tent with six of my grandchildren, ages eleven down to four. Beth prepared a special breakfast when we got up. At the time of this writing, we have had a sleepover for thirty-three straight months. Although some of the cold months, we slept in the house not in the tent! God and family!

The weekend before we left for Romania, our daughter Kari and her husband Zach hosted a birthday party for their three children, two born in July and one on August first. What a special family gathering. We didn't know how special at the time. Beth and I had a beautiful picture taken with all eleven of our grandchildren. Again, what matters most is God and family!

REFUGE REFLECTIONS

1. Is the Great Commission in Matthew 28:18–20 only for those seasons where life is calm and the storms of life are not raging?

2. If we rely on our strength most days, the storms of life seem too fierce to have time to make disciples. Remember the 4 Ps of the Great Commision. Jesus promises us his Power, "All authority on heaven and earth has been given to me" and his Presence, "And surely I will be with you always, to the very end of the age."

3. Beth and I discovered that in the fiercest of storms the Lord's power and presence allowed us to touch people in incredible places with his love. Are you open to be used in the storms of life or are you focused on "Why me?"

4. When Beth and I were aware of his Presence and open to his Power, we were used for his Purpose and we received a Peace we could have never imagined. You can too!

CHAPTER 19

Go Big and Go Home

We were so looking forward to our mission trip to Romania. This would be Beth's sixth trip, fourth with cancer. My journal entry days before we would leave was from Hebrews 12:2–3, "Let us run with perseverance the race marked out for us fixing our eyes on Jesus, the pioneer and perfecter of our faith. For the joy set before him he endured the cross!" This verse really puts our struggles and storms of life into perspective. The Son of God joyfully endured the torture and death on the cross for us! Beth and I with our eyes fixed on Jesus were going to keep running the race marked out for us!

Beth completed her fourth cycle of chemo in Grand Rapids. This was the second cycle in a row where Beth received the complete chemo and had no transfusions. A week before our trip to Romania we were blindsided with the news that Beth's cancer numbers were starting to increase. After almost five years in this TSW/cancer storm, we had more and more learned to focus on Jesus not on the ever-changing waves, no matter how menacing they could seem.

I was concerned and asked our doctor if Beth should go to Romania. He said her body had to have time to clear the chemo from the last cycle. Even if she was home and not in Romania, she would not be receiving treatment for a few weeks. He planned to start a new chemo in August when we got back. He also felt encouraged that Beth would qualify for the experimental treatment at the University of Michigan now that her cancer numbers were much reduced since January.

I didn't tell Beth, but I wondered if Beth maybe shouldn't go to Romania. She had avoided taking any pain pills except Tylenol for the last five years. Beginning in July, she was experiencing such intense pain that she was taking Tramadol to fall asleep. I was concerned! Beth was not going to miss serving with both her daughters and me this year!

The next day, after getting the news about Beth's cancer numbers, I told her I didn't care if our bedroom was staged in our lake house. I wanted to move our bedroom set into our duplex. I felt if Beth didn't have much time she should not be sleeping on a mattress on the floor.

Before moving our bedroom set, I painted one of our walls an accent orange like our master bedroom in the house we were selling. For the week before we left for Romania our bedroom was fully decorated with wall hangings, window treatments, and furniture. I got to see those beautiful green eyes twinkle.

Beth had an early morning doctor's appointment the day before we would leave for Romania. Her blood test numbers were great, and we were ready to go! Around noon Beth told me her abdomen was really hurting and she should have said something at her appointment.

We went back to the cancer center late that afternoon and they ordered a CAT scan to rule out a blood clot. There was no blood clot, but Beth's spleen was enlarged. The physician's assistant said this was a common reaction to chemo. She would order steroid pills for Beth to take while we were in Romania.

We were going to Romania! I imagine most people, if they had known about Beth's abdominal pain, would have considered Beth and I out of our minds! Yes, we were sold out for Jesus! We had really lived this way for the last three years. Actually, we had lived this way for the last forty years.

When Beth and I decided to sell a successful dental practice and move out of state with four small children to attend seminary, many people were shaking their heads. A good friend and neighbor suggested that I make an appointment with a counselor. He was a member of our church. We were looking to the Lord. The storm we were in was not about us. The storm had blown us to places and in contact with people we would have never come in contact with so that we could share our faith!

With Beth in considerable pain, I was running around finishing packing and getting ready to leave for the airport with the girls in the morning. My precious angel Beth said, "Sit with me, please; the pain is really bad!" Only a couple of times in the last five years did I see the glint in her beautiful green eyes somewhat dimmed. Beth's eyes were still sparkling, but as the song goes, she needed to "Just Be Held!" As we sat together, I was overwhelmed with over forty years of "for better or for worse, for richer for poor, in sickness, and in health." It wasn't where we were or what we were doing. It was that Beth and I were together and we were holding each other, allowing the Lord to hold us in his loving arms!

The next morning, we loaded up the van and my beautiful girls and I headed to the airport. Beth's pain was tolerable as we boarded the plane in Detroit. We learned so many things during this cancer/TSW experience. My quiet graced-filled servant wife had to learn how to ask for help and to admit when she needed help. We both were brought up with the "work hard, I can do it myself" life ethics. I remembered when I gently told Beth, "Don't rob others of the blessing of serving you!" She took those words to heart!

Beth's knee and back pain were to the point that Beth asked if she could be wheeled through the long terminal in Frankfurt in a wheelchair. We were wheeled straight to the gate for our connection to Romania. Once Beth was settled at our gate, I went back to find Kari and Kristi. They were stuck in a security line and it was obvious they would miss our connection.

I told the girls something I would tell Beth from time to time, "Play the "C" card!" Sometimes, because of Beth's cancer, you needed extra help. Don't be afraid to ask for it. I told the girls to tell people in line ahead of them that their elderly mother with health problems was at the gate and ask if they would kindly let them cut in line so they didn't miss the flight. It worked! Many people allowed them to cut in line and they just barely made our flight!

Our mission team, due to flight delays, did not arrive in Sigishoara until almost midnight Romania time. I will never forget when Beth got off the bus and had to walk up a short hill to the entrance to the church. She was so out of breath walking slowly she had to stop and rest about every twenty feet.

Eric, our physician from Arkansas, injured his back a few weeks prior to our trip. With faith in the Lord, he, like Beth, came on our trip. He was also moving pretty slow after all those flight hours from the United States.

The next morning our team would split up and worship in four different village churches. Last year I encouraged Beth to take advantage of the platform cancer had given her to share her faith. She gave a short testimonial last year. This year she was planning on giving her testimonial.

In the weeks leading up to our trip, every time I tried to give her advice, she would put me off and say she had it under control. I was the experienced public speaker, and she was the gentle, under the radar soul. Our daughter Kari went with her to a village church and Beth gave an over sixteen-minute testimonial of living her faith in the storm of cancer. Kari videoed the entire testimonial on her phone.

Beth opened her testimonial by saying, "Do you know in Matthew where it says go and make disciples of all nations? It doesn't say go when your children are out of the house and they are all grown up, or when your bills are paid, your house is all in order, or you feel good. He said GO and he meant NOW!" Beth then went on to tell her five-year journey with TSW and cancer. Little did we know at the time, the impact Beth's testimonial would have in the days ahead.

This was Kristi's fourth trip to Romania, three after beating cancer herself! She gave her testimonial in another village church. Being a pianist, she sang a song as part of her testimonial. I shared the message in another of the churches. Every year I was given the humble privilege of bringing the message to one of the Romanian churches we ministered alongside.

The last few mission trips our hotel had not been able to accommodate our entire team together for evening dinner. This tended to split up our group and affect our ability to meet each night for team devotions and prayer. Last year was one of the more frustrating trips I had ever been a part of. Satan seemed to really attack us. The feeling of coming together for a common mission just wasn't the same last year.

Feeling this way about last year and after much prayer I contacted a member of the 2018 team and veteran of probably twenty mission trips, James. My dear friend from South Carolina and I talked in March, and I asked him if he felt something was different or something missing in our 2018 team. He mentioned two words that were truly a God-inspired observation. He felt we were about "TASKS and not MINISTRY!"

He hit the nail on the head. We were expending a lot of energy and effort doing tasks, but we were not being Spirit led! I thanked him and began to pray about how to move our group from accomplishing tasks to being instruments of God to bring the life-changing message of the gospel to the lost.

On our mission team the members doing triage were taking health histories and blood pressure. The members in optical were passing out glasses. In dental we were extracting

teeth. The medical team members were doing exams and prescribing meds. In pharmacy they were obviously dispensing medications. I think subconsciously we felt the real ministry was being done with adults who went through evangelism and with children in children's ministry only.

Our American and Romanian mission team members gathered

on the first Sunday night for dinner, followed by a meeting to prepare for the five villages we would visit Monday through Friday. I led a time of devotion and prayer. I encouraged our team to not be about tasks but about ministry. My encouragement was that no matter the role we filled, that we would be open to God moments and opportunities to spiritually connect.

On previous mission trips it was difficult to get everyone together before loading supplies and getting on the bus for the village of the day. This year I arranged in advance for a member of our team each day to lead a devotional on the bus. After the devotion time I then had song sheets and a speaker that hooked to my phone to play music. We sang two songs of praise on the bus each morning.

Steve, our leader, would then lead us in prayer before we got off the bus and began to unload and set up in the village of the day. In addition, we found a prayer partner for the week from our team, someone we didn't know well! Each night we ate dinner with not just our American team members; this year we were joined with our Romanian team members. Each evening I led a time of devotion prior to our team meeting.

Beth and our beautiful daughters were together serving in triage. My girls were radiating the love of Jesus that was in their hearts as they welcomed villagers. They, along with their translators, took health histories on all the villagers along with blood pressures. The girls would write down all the needs of the people and where they needed to go. I truly believe this was the most meaningful, blessed, uplifting, encouraging experience Beth and I shared with our daughters in our lifetime. When I had a break in the dental clinic, I would briefly visit them. My three beautiful girls were glowing, exuding the love of Jesus!

I remember when Kristi was on her first trip. A few days into the trip I knew I didn't need to ask her if she would be returning to Romania. This was Kristi's fourth trip, the third since beating cancer! The same thing was happening with Kari on this trip. The daughter who never really wanted to go was also blown away by the experience and was most definitely returning.

I can't come up with words to describe how spiritually moving this trip was, not only for my family, but also for the entire team. We have always had great translators, but this year we were connected in a very special way. Nights that we were free to roam the historic city of Sighisoara, our translators who were sixteen to maybe twenty-two years of age wanted to be with us.

This was the first year our dinner and devotion time each night included our Romanian brothers and sisters in Christ. In the past they would go home to be with their families. I truly believe this extra time eating together and spending time in devotions with each other was how the Spirit brought us together in a very special way.

When we got back to our hotel Wednesday night, I saw Beth was writing a note. The next morning, she gave one of our translators Debora a note and told her to give it to her mom. On Friday morning Debora told Beth her mom couldn't read English, so she had to translate the note from Beth to her mom. Debora was in tears and was hugging Beth.

My quiet grace-filled wife, in the midst of her cancer storm, encouraged dear Debora and her mom by telling her what a kind, gracious servant Debora was and how God was going to mightily use Debora in the years ahead. I can still see sweet Debora as we were on the bus waiting to leave our last village on Friday. Dear Debora was pushing one of the villagers home in a wheelchair down a dirt road.

By Wednesday the steroids were definitely helping with Beth's abdominal pain, but Beth still couldn't walk up the hill to explore all the shops and stores in the walled city of Sigishoara. I decided to borrow a wheelchair from the church. I prided myself on being in great physical shape. The incline was so steep into the walled city that I was only able to push Beth halfway before sadly giving up.

Each clinic day went so smoothly until Friday, our last day. The way in which we set up made it easy for villagers to cut by triage and get in line for the doctor or dentists. By cutting, the villagers would not be directed to evangelism first! As complications go it was really minor. We blocked an opening off with a table and moved the chairs where people would sit to wait.

On the bus back to our hotel that night, I gently let our leader Steve know that it was his fault we had the time of confusion that morning. He looked at me quizzically. I informed him that it was his fault because it was the only morning that he had rushed off the bus without leading the team in prayer! Only God knows, but I don't think it was a coincidence!

After the last clinic day on Friday night, we always had a dinner and a time for us Americans to thank and honor our Romanian translators. This year was so special. I asked my translator Jonathon and three other youth to teach me the refrain of the song "Holy, Holy, Holy" in Romanian.

Together we led our combined team in worship. I joined in on the refrain! It was such a moving evening. As tired as we were after a long week, no one wanted to leave. We just couldn't quit praising the God who died for us and empowered our week of ministry. We sang the songs "Our God", "What A Wonderful Name", and "I Am."

We closed with the song "How Great Is Our God" and we sang the refrain in both English and Romanian at the same time. I don't know what it will be like in heaven someday, but I know we all got a sample. I am shivering as I reminisce about the worship. I had my arm around my sweetheart with her hands raised high in praise. Surrounded by my beautiful daughters, there is no greater feeling for a parent than to witness their children mightily serving and praising the Lord. What an amazing week!

The next day I felt like I witnessed a true miracle by God. Beth could barely walk a hundred feet up the hill to the church the night we arrived. A week later my courageous wife spent all day touring the city of Sigishoara and walked all the way up to the historic church on the top of the hill. Our dear Dr. Eric with his ruptured disk in his back also had an unbelievable week.

When you answer the call of the Lord, responding with the

words of Isaiah in Isaiah 6:8, "Here I am Lord, send me," God will give you the strength to serve him. He will truly equip you for service. God truly empowered Beth for her to be on this trip! With God nothing is impossible.

We arranged to spend two days in Germany on the way back to the US. Both Beth and I are virtually 100 percent German descent. We spent two days in the city of Cologne. There is a cathedral in Cologne that is much bigger than Notre Dame in Paris. The construction of this cathedral started in AD 1248. Wow! I got up early our second day and did my morning devotion time in this amazing cathedral.

We relaxed on a river cruise one afternoon and also took a bus tour of the town. Beth is an amazing cook who loves making German recipes passed down for generations. I was so blessed to see those green eyes sparkle as she tasted the German cuisine and enjoyed the desserts.

Shortly after Beth started this five-year TSW/cancer storm I hung a plaque in our entrance way with a message of Vivian Green that we lived by, "Life isn't about waiting for the storm to pass … it's learning to dance in the rain." My three girls and I were sure dancing! Little did my sweet daughters and I know how deeply we would treasure the memories of this mission trip in Romania and side trip to Germany!

We didn't need jet fuel on the flight home from Frankfurt. My three Knoerr girls and I were so blessed by the experience of the mission trip together, along with our time in Germany, we could have floated home. With the seven-hour time difference between Michigan and Romania, needless to say, we woke up very early on August 1 in our bed in Grand Rapids. I got up and drove to Marshall to close out our bank accounts, pick up mail and transfer our mail to our new address in Grand Rapids, instead of going with Beth to her doctor appointment.

Beth had blood tests while I was driving to Marshall. We anticipated she would have IV chemo the next day which was

Friday. I was at the bank when Beth called me. She was weeping uncontrollably. I could hardly understand what she was trying to tell me. Apparently, her blood tests indicated that her cancer was really bad. I definitely broke speed limits getting home. We spent the evening lying in each other's arms and in the Lord's arms.

We went to chemo the next day and I tried to get our nurse to explain to me what was going on. All she would say was that Beth's cancer numbers were really not good. Beth started her new IV chemo and they gave her an anti-nausea medication. We did what we always did during chemo. We read our Bibles for all to see! I prayed for a miracle like I had been doing for over three years.

We decided to go out to dinner at one of Beth's favorite restaurants, Panera Bread. I took a cute picture of the two of us. I will treasure this picture forever. We then went shopping at Hobby Lobby, one of Beth's favorite places. Over the years I had collected a lot of mementos in Romania and I wanted to hang them on the wall in my new study. My sweetheart helped me find the perfect shelf for the Romania wall.

Through the night Beth experienced extreme cramping and constipation from the anti-nausea medication. The laxative didn't really help until midmorning on Saturday. My dear wife was experiencing another menacing wave in the storm. I finally got Beth to sleep in the early morning hours.

As I was waiting for Beth to wake up, I watched the video of her Romania testimonial. I wrote MIRACLE, MIRACLE, MIRACLE, you're not done with Beth yet, in my journal. As Saturday progressed Beth seemed to be getting more and more tired and quiet. I left her for a short time and went to the grocery store and brought her back flowers. She still had the sparkle in her eye when I gave her the flowers, but she was very quiet. I assumed this new chemo treatment was causing Beth's lethargy.

On Sunday we decided not to go to church but to watch it online. Beth was extremely weary and very achy. I was thinking to myself, "If this new chemo treatment is going be this bad there is no way I can consider working even part time. Before leaving for Romania, I had interviewed for a one day per week job as a dentist at the county jail.

Late afternoon Kristi came over and was very concerned about how weak her mom was acting. She asked if I should call the doctor. I told her we had an appointment early the next day. About 9:00 p.m. I basically had to carry Beth to the bathroom. I called Kristi and asked her to go with me to take her mom to emergency. I had to carry Beth out to our minivan, she was so limp she couldn't walk.

By the time we wheeled her into emergency, Beth was unresponsive. Her blood pressure had dropped to 60/40. It looked like an episode of the TV show ER. Doctors and nurses rushing around, in and out of Beth's room trying to keep her from slipping away. They gave her IV meds to stabilize her and intubated her to assist with breathing.

I called all our children and they all headed to the hospital. Blood tests showed very high white cell level. The ER staff felt she had a bad infection. I knew the high numbers were cancer cells. The CT scan also showed lesions on Beth's liver, rectum, and spleen. I didn't tell my kids, but I knew it was bad.

They transferred Beth to a local hospital at 2:00 a.m. By the time we got there, her catheter bag was full of blood. Beth was also bleeding internally. All my children and spouses were now arriving at the hospital. When morning came Beth was still unresponsive but stable. My two youngest sons and spouses decided to go home.

Over the last five years, through the storms of TSW/cancer the Lord had blown us off the course of our normal life into places we would never have gone on our own. We were now on a mission trip to the patients and staff of Blodgett Hospital. As I prayed early Monday morning my journal reflection was, "Help me share our story so others at Blodgett Hospital can come to know you as Savior. Please heal Beth, please dear Jesus!"

By late afternoon, my good friend from church, Dave, drove over from Marshall and prayed with me. Just minutes after Dave left, the doctor at Blodgett who had consulted with Dr. Brinker, Beth's oncologist, wanted to talk with me. In their professional judgment there was nothing medically they could do to beat back the cancer!

They could keep Beth on meds, and she may live a few days. I shared the news with my sweet girls, and we were all at peace that Beth would have wanted us to let her go home to heaven. The medical team felt if they discontinued the sedative and removed the ventilator, Beth may wake up and we could say our goodbyes to her.

At 8:00 p.m., with our Casting Crowns music playing in the background for all the staff to hear, our family of twenty-three gathered around Beth to say goodbye. My nine-year-old grandson Caleb wouldn't leave his grandma's side, sitting next to her bed holding her hand. I sat next to Beth and Liam, my six-year-old grandson sat on my lap hugging me chest to chest. About 9:00 p.m. I decided to get in bed next to Beth and put my arm around her. The Casting Crowns song "Just Be Held" had ministered to us for over four years. That's all I could do now was hold my honey and allow God to hold the two of us like he had done for over forty years.

I woke up about 5:00 a.m., obviously everyone had left while I fell asleep holding my sweetheart. I got out of bed and realized I probably needed to let the world through Facebook know that Beth's time was short. Just as I posted on Facebook, the nurse came in and said Beth's blood pressure and respiration were dropping. He told me I may want to call any loved ones. As soon as I got off the phone with Kari and Kristi, he said it's now.

I will always remember this moment. I kissed Beth lightly, stroked her forehead, took her hand, and gently whispered to my beautiful sweetheart, "Beth I will spend the rest of my life trying to get as many people into heaven with you as I can!" Beth was opening her eyes in heaven. My honey girl did indeed "Go Big and Go Home" to heaven!

REFUGE REFLECTIONS

1. Do we in life get so caught up in going through the motions and checking off the tasks on our lists that we miss the personal connections that God intends in our marriages, our families, our neighborhoods, and even our churches?

2. How can you see the items on your "to-do" list as opportunities for spiritual connections and potential "God moments?"

3. As you shift from a "tasks" mentality as a spouse, parent, or adult child, to a "ministry" mentality be prepared for new and abundant spiritual connections and relationships!

CHAPTER 20

BE The Hope

A few hours after Beth opened her eyes in heaven our big family, except Rod's family, met at the Cracker Barrel restaurant to honor the ultimate hostess with a big family breakfast. Rod and Danielle arrived shortly after we got to my house. Pastor Kris, from Beth and my church in Marshall arrived a few minutes later and prayed with our family and we watched Beth's Romania video testimonial with all my children and Pastor Kris and had a good "cry!"

The next day was our grandson Kaden's seventh birthday. If Beth had any influence with the Lord, I am sure she didn't want to pass away on one of her precious grandchild's birthdays. So, she opened her eyes in heaven the day before. Our whole family gathered at Kari and Zach's house. The week before our Romania trip, we all were gathered at Kari and Zach's as a family, not knowing it would be the last time with Beth. That picture with our grandkids that day was the last picture with Beth.

After forty years of sleeping next to Beth, I can't tell you how many times I would wake up in the night in the days and weeks following her opening those beautiful green eyes in heaven. I began to do what worked for Beth when she couldn't fall asleep.

I started praying the ABC prayer of thanksgiving every time I woke up in the night. Beth and I had learned the importance of focusing on our blessings and thanksgiving during the storm of cancer. I was so blessed by my family. Gratitude worked again; it took my focus off the new storm of my loss. I was blessed by so many people who wrote notes, called, messaged and visited. I was really loved on!

My sweetheart in heaven even wrote me notes. I was looking at the blank wall over our fireplace in the new duplex thinking I needed to put a picture of Beth and me over the mantle. The next day I found a to-do list Beth made for when she got back from Romania. She was one organized woman! A mother of five and grandmother of eleven had to be!

Her checklist said to put "The Lord Bless You" picture over the fireplace. Numbers 6:24–27 was the basis for the message at our wedding and really our life together. We had this wall hanging in our master bathroom at our lake house. Beth from heaven was telling me to put the words, "The Lord bless you and keep you. The Lord make His face shine upon you and be gracious to you. The Lord look upon you with favor and give you peace" over the fireplace.

I also found a note that Beth must have written to me the day after we got back from Romania when she got the tidal wave news about her cancer.

For I KNOW THE PLANS *I have for you*,
DECLARES THE *Lord*, PLANS TO PROSPER
YOU AND NOT TO HARM YOU, PLANS
TO *give you hope* AND A FUTURE.

JEREMIAH 29:11

Dear Rod,
I can't tell you how much I have loved you throughout our 40+ years of being together.
Thank you for everything! You are truly a man of God. I know you will succeed in all you do with your new business. Thank you for taking such good care of me during my sick times. I only wish that our "living the dream" could have lasted longer. Continue to love on our children + grands. Remind them often how much I loved them. Carry on our family traditions. I love you so much. This is a hard + not so fun note to be writing! I will

I can't imagine the tears that were flowing as my honey wrote that note. Beth was saying your job is to love our family for her and me! That is what Beth would have done if I were in heaven first. A couple of nights later I had the first sleepover with my grandkids in the tent without Beth. In the morning I made scrambled eggs and donut holes just like Grandma Beth would have done ... carrying on our family traditions!

A week later, grandsons Calvin, age eleven, and Caleb, age nine, were riding with me to Marshall to mow the camp lawn. They were squabbling like brothers when I said to them, "What Would

Gramma Do?" My response sounded like the saying, "What Would Jesus Do?" that spawned the WWJD rubber bracelets.

That thought created the idea of bracelets with WWGD to honor their grandma. I told the boys we would order the bracelets for all the grandchildren and future grandchildren. I ordered the bracelets obviously in Beth's color, pink. I told the boys to keep it a secret until we could give them out at the same time. Caleb was so excited with the idea the surprise element was killing him.

A few days after Beth went to heaven, I wrote 1 Corinthians 4:2 in my journal, "Those who have been given a trust must prove faithful!" The next day I journaled Beth's life verse Jeremiah 29:11, "I know the plans I have for your declares Lord. Plans to prosper you and not harm you. Plans to give you hope and a future" and my new life verse Romans 15:13, "May the God of hope fill you with all joy and peace as you trust in him, so that you may overflow with hope by the power of the Holy Spirit." I also wrote my thought of a Bethehope logo. In big letters I wrote give me a MEGAVISION, YOUR VISION!"

I looked up the online business card company, Vistaprint. I emailed my ideas for a Bethehope logo. I never verbally talked to anyone, but after a few back-and-forth emails, a business card that was in Beth's favorite color pink was created. The T of Beth's name was the cross of Jesus and the designer made it look like waves of light were emanating from the cross. The designer must have been a person of faith. I also put Beth's life verse, Jeremiah 29:11 on the card. I ordered not only a box of 500 cards but also a 3ft x 8ft banner. The picture of Beth's name that God gave me in January was becoming a reality.

I had watched my father-in-law for over thirty years love and adore his dear honey, Martha. At his funeral, I had the opportunity to share a few words. There were two words that perfectly described how he felt toward Mom. He cherished and adored Mom! I put Dad's cane by our exterior door the night of his funeral so I would daily be reminded of the godly example of a husband with a servant heart who cherished and adored his dear wife.

After sixty years of marriage, Mom Fritzler passed away. Dad did not quit living. As much as Dad adored Mom, for the next six years he loved his family, served at his church until the day God called him home. I looked at Dad's cane and knew I too needed to honor how Beth lived her life in service to her Savior. That day I began a new tradition. Each morning I would say, "Lord how can I Bethehope to someone today?" Each evening I would ask myself, "How did I Bethehope to someone today?"

The girls and I decided to wait until the last Saturday in September to have Beth's Celebration of Life service and dinner. This was over six weeks after Beth's passing. We felt it would allow more people to come to the gathering.

We planned to have the service and dinner in Marshall at the church, Family Bible, which Beth and I called home. We posted an invitation on Facebook to Beth's day and asked people to RSVP. We were overwhelmed by the response. We needed to plan for about 300 people. We needed to find another place that could accommodate more people.

God already knew the plan. When we left for Romania, we had planned on hosting the tenth annual Knoerr pig roast in Grand Rapids in August or September. New plan … Beth's Celebration of Life dinner would also be the tenth annual pig roast and we would rent a large tent and host it at the camp!

In the weeks leading up to Beth's Celebration of Life service I was having difficulty falling back to sleep at night. The Bible verse Ecclesiastes 4:12 that is often referred to at weddings, "A cord of three strands is not easily broken" came to mind. The symbolism of this verse is that the three cords are husband, wife, and God. With God at the center of a marriage there is nothing that can break the union. I was feeling down, and that verse made me realize that Beth was still one of the cords, even if she was in heaven. God was not turning his back on me. The only way the cord would be broken is if I fell from the faith. I drew great strength and encouragement from that verse.

Throughout Beth's health challenges, together we strove to live out the exhortation of Hebrews 12:1–2, "…let us throw off everything that hinders and the sin that so easily entangles. And let us run with perseverance the race marked out for us, fixing our eyes on Jesus!" I was fixing my eyes on Jesus and I was trying to run the new race marked out for me, but it wasn't the same without Beth. Then I read the beginning words of verse 1, "Therefore since we are surrounded by such a great cloud of witnesses." The great cloud of witnesses was referring to all those who had died in the faith and were now in heaven. Beth was one of those witnesses! I realized Beth was a cheerleader up in heaven saying Bethehope, Bethehope, Bethehope!

Beth's Celebration of Life service had the potential of bringing great hope to all in attendance if the spiritual journey God had taken us on as we lived through the storm of TSW and cancer could be shared. The only person who could truly speak about the journey was me. With Beth as my heavenly cheerleader, I called Pastor Kris and asked him if I could lead the service. His answer was, "I figured that is what you would want to do!"

A big part of sharing our journey was for us to sing the songs that ministered to the depth of our souls. I wanted to ask my friend Matt to be the worship leader for Beth's service. Matt was a guitarist and had led worship at times at Family Bible. He was one of my fellow Fight Club leaders.

Matt's wife Michelle was one of the young moms that Beth hosted each month. In addition. Michelle had been dealing with issues of vertigo the last few years and had to take a break as a schoolteacher. She had just accepted a teaching job in the fall. After years of living in the storm of vertigo while trying to be a mom to three children and wife, she was excited to be getting back to teaching.

In July, while we were in Romania, Michelle was diagnosed with breast cancer! Because of the technology of the internet and Facebook, I was able to pray with Matt and Michelle shortly after her cancer diagnosis from Romania on facetime. Due to the storms that our marriages had endured and grown through, Beth and I were very close to Matt and his wife Michelle.

Any reasonable person would have felt there was no way I could hold it together and share the message at Beth's Celebration of Life service. Same with Matt, with our close friendship and with the recent news of his wife Michelle's cancer, how could he lead worship for someone who had just died of cancer. God knew exactly what he was doing!

As I was cleaning out a dresser drawer a few days before Beth's service, I came across a few pages she had written to our children and left on our bed the first time she went to Romania. The note basically said that if you are reading this something happened to Dad and I in Romania. She then wrote a personal note of appreciation and spiritual encouragement to each of our five children and to each of our grandchildren that were living in 2014.

I love the message my sweetheart wanted to share if she was being taken to heaven. My children were so blessed when I shared this with them!

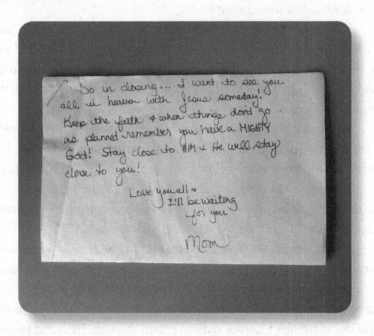

So in closing... I want to see you all in heaven with Jesus someday! Keep the faith & when things don't go as planned remember you have a MIGHTY God! Stay close to HIM & He will stay close to you!

Love you all & I'll be waiting for you

Mom

Back around Thanksgiving last year Beth made two entries in her journal, "I really need a miracle," and "I love my babies so much and I want them to BE THERE!" About a month after Beth was in heaven, I found a box up on the closet shelf. I was truly blown away by what I found. There were little cloth bags with labels for me, my sons and sons-in-law and all my grandsons. Then I found little delicately gift-wrapped gift boxes with bows. One for each daughter, daughter-in-law, and granddaughter. Leave it to Beth to make the girls gifts much fancier than the boys. Beth also had a couple extra boy and girl gifts. Beth was always a planner; she knew there may be more grandbabies!

When I opened one of the gifts my tears wouldn't stop flowing.

There was a bracelet in each gift bag and box with the words, "Be There" engraved on each bracelet. I could tell over the last six months that Beth felt her time was drawing near. With her last acts of service, she wanted to impress on her precious family what was most important to her! She wanted all her babies in heaven one day! Notice the first four letters of those two words spell Beth! At the time I was trying to decide when to present these gifts from Beth.

The morning of Beth's Celebration of Life Day my prayer was that those present would see that any strength or encouragement Beth and I demonstrated to others was not us. We were two regular people caught in the storms of life. I hoped to take people on the journey Beth and I traveled. As I prayed that morning that Beth and my stormy journey would Bethehope to all in attendance.

As I thought back to our wedding day forty years ago the words of our traditional wedding vows took on a much deeper meaning. "I, Rod take thee, Beth, to by my wedded wife, to have and to hold from this day forward, for better, for worse, for richer, for poorer, in sickness and in health, to love and to cherish, till death do us part!"

Many married couples, when deluged by the storms of life, find themselves drifting apart in their relationship with the Lord and also with each other. Our love for the Lord and for each other grew more and more intensely intimate during the last five years of our marriage when due to the storms of life we were experiencing the worse, poorer, sickness not the better, richer, health of our wedding vows. This does not make sense from an earthly perspective. From an eternal perspective the worst five years of our marriage were the best five years of our marriage.

Pastor Kris led off Beth's Celebration of Life service by reading the words of hope from 1Thessalonians 4:13–14, "Brothers and sisters, we do not want you to be uninformed about those who sleep in death, so that you do not grieve like the rest of mankind, who have no hope. For we believe Jesus died and rose again, and so we believe that God will bring with Jesus those who have fallen asleep in Him." We indeed did not grieve like others because Beth opened her eyes in heaven knowing the only thing and person that mattered, Only Jesus! My sweetheart was experiencing heaven with our Lord and Savior!

We then opened by singing the song "Only Jesus." Everything Beth and I experienced was because of Jesus! Any impact or encouragement we had on others was not Rod and Beth. The hope we had and shared was because we knew all that mattered was "Only Jesus!"

"I don't want to leave a legacy, Only Jesus, I've only got one life to live, I'll let every second point to Him, Only Jesus"

... Did I live the truth to the ones I love? Was my life the proof there is only One whose name will last forever?

Our love for each other and our desire to cherish each other was never greater. That doesn't make earthly sense. As we grew in our faith and marriage we began to realize, "It wasn't about us!" Wherever the storms of life blew us, we found opportunities to be the hope to others. What we began to realize was that people, due to Beth's cancer, expected us to be depressed or angry with God. When we weren't it only made our message of grace and faith more powerful.

Our second song was "Just Be Held." The words of this song drew us closer to the arms of our loving Lord and each other!

"So when you're on your knees and answers seem so far away, You're not alone, stop holding on and just be held, Your worlds not falling apart, it's falling into place, I'm on the throne, stop holding on and just be held"

"If your eyes are on the storm, You'll wonder if I love you still, But if your eyes are on the cross, You'll know I always have and always will"

During the TSW/cancer journey Beth and I grew so close. As I slowed down, I learned it was the simple things in life that mattered. The year before the storm of TSW/cancer blew in I experienced my first ten-week Fight Club. One of the assignments during that chapter was to leave short sticky notes of appreciation around the house.

Because of that assignment, since then I would regularly leave short notes of appreciation or sticky notes for Beth around the house. Instead of birthday cards, I would write a note of appreciation! My encouragement to all in attendance is that you often don't realize the impact of taking a few minutes to encourage. I then held up a three-ring binder. Beth had saved every loving note and encouraging sticky note!

The third song for Beth's service, also by Casting Crowns was "Praise You in This Storm."

"And I will lift my hands, For you are who you are, No matter where I am, And every tear I've cried, You hold in Your hand, You never left my side, And though my heart is torn, I will praise You in this storm"

I sang this song with both my arms raised to the heavens with tears streaming down my cheeks. In the last few years as my honey was journeying in the storm toward heaven, my quiet, gentle, wife raised her arms higher and higher in worship as the waves of the storms grew higher and more intense.

We then showed a portion of Beth's Romanian testimonial. Yes, my soft-spoken Beth spoke at her own Celebration of Life service or I should say God spoke through Beth. My sweetheart must have known she was dying because this quiet behind-the-scenes servant of God boldly and confidently spoke to the people in Romania and to all assembled.

As Beth was closing her testimonial, she said, "When you are in the storms of life, just go, listen to God and go, he has me in his hands he has you in his hands." She then closed with her life verse Jeremiah 29:11, "I know the plans I have for you declare the Lord. Plans to prosper you and not to harm you. Plans to give you hope and a future."

If Beth and I could grow to live John 9:3 in the storms of life so could they. "This happened so that the works of God could be displayed through him, (us)." I told them my grandchildren would be passing out Bethehope cards as they left church!

We closed with the song Beth had made her ring tone on her phone for the last few months of her life, "I Can Only Imagine!" by Mercy Me. And by the way, God mightily held Matt and I together as we had the privilege of being used mightily by God!

So many people stayed for the pig roast/Celebration of Life dinner. We hosted this dinner every year as a way to thank the Lord for all our blessings and as a way to share our blessings with family and friends. It was a tradition for me to open with prayer. Prior to the prayer I had a surprise for all assembled. All in attendance got to witness Beth's last message to her beloved babies, as my family opened their gifts, the BE THERE bracelets!

I had a large BETheHope banner with a pink background (Beth's favorite color) on the wall behind the food table. It was my prayer that the testimonial of Beth and my journey would encourage those who shared Beth's Celebration of Life Day to see their lives as opportunities especially in the storms of life to BE The Hope!

I have framed my last words to Beth as she was opening those sparkling green eyes in heaven. Every time as I sat down to write this book, I would recite that commitment. Until God calls me home to heaven, I will see every day as an opportunity to live my last words to Beth.

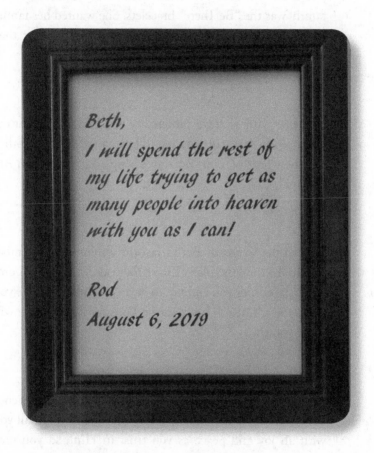

Beth,
I will spend the rest of my life trying to get as many people into heaven with you as I can!

Rod
August 6, 2019

REFUGE REFLECTIONS

1. If you knew you had months to live, would it change how you lived and your priorities? Beth's last statement to her family was the "Be There" bracelets. She wanted her family to know the most important thing to her was that they would one day spend eternity in heaven.

2. Are you trying to leave a monetary or a career legacy at the expense of what truly matters? How can you begin to live out the words of Tim McGraw's song, "Live Like You Are Dying?"

3. Believe the words of Beth's favorite Bible verse, Jeremiah 29:11, "I know the plans I have for you declares the Lord, plans to prosper you and not to harm you, plans to give you hope and a future." Look to the Lord for help and he will show you the way!

4. As you seek the Lord and trust in Him you will experience the words of Romans 15:13, "May the God of hope fill you with all joy and peace as you trust in Him, so you may overflow with hope by the power of the Holy Spirit!"

EPILOGUE

The Rainbow Following the Storm

Beth and I discovered in the storms of life that if we served and encouraged others, God in return blessed us and we did indeed find a purpose in the midst of the cancer storm. We grew individually and as a couple in the midst of the storm. I have been forever changed as a result of the journey Beth and I traveled.

I am in the process of forming a 501c3 organization, Bethehope. My vision is so multifaceted that the perfect word to describe it is a "Rainbow"! This world is in need of HOPE and my vision is like a multicolored Rainbow

1. Bethehope Purpose Groups

A couple of months after Beth opened her eyes in heaven, I attended a ten-week grief support group. I found this to be very helpful for the early stage of my grieving. As I entered the New Year of 2020, I decided to attend the new ten-week support group again. I went to the first grief support night. At the end of the session, I realized I didn't need a "support" group, I needed a group that would help answer the "now what" question.

I decided then that I would start a group to help those who have lost loved ones discover their purpose. My Bethehope group has been meeting for almost 2 years. It is a "purpose" group, not a "support" group. I have a vision of Bethehope purpose groups for people experiencing any storm of life. People experiencing health challenges, marital, financial, or work storms need to find purpose in the storm!

2. Bethehope Coaching

Sometimes the storms of life are so intense that being a part of a purpose group is not enough. In the midst of Beths's TSW/cancer storm I became certified as a leadership/life coach with the John Maxwell Team. I will be offering individual, couples, and family coaching under the Bethehope 501c3 umbrella.

3. Bethehope Speaking and Seminars

I plan to utilize my public speaking experience to bring the message of hope and purpose in the midst of life's storms to organizations, churches, and schools.

4. Bethehope Retreat

The camp that Beth and I took a leap of faith on and purchased in the middle of her cancer journey will officially open in 2022. It is my vision that BeTheHope Retreat can be a place where churches, schools, organizations and purpose groups of all kinds can meet. Beth's legacy of hospitality and hope will continue in the years ahead.

5. Bethehope Facebook Group

For years I have felt the media has become more and more negative and divisive. I have always wished there was a station or channel that just showed all the simple acts of kindness people did every day. I created a Facebook group with one purpose to be a forum where people can post the Bethehope moments they choose to experience with people around them. Our country and world will not be changed by government or church "programs". Let's encourage others and grow this group to millions and change the world through simple Bethehope connections!

6. Bethehope movie

Be on the lookout for this movie. My last words to Beth as she opened her eyes in heaven were, "I will spend the rest of my life getting as many people into heaven with you as I can!" I believe God has a Bethehope movie that the world must view. The movie will echo Beth's faith encouragements from her testimonial two weeks before she opened her eyes in heaven.

My gentle sweetheart in that Romanian village asked, "Do you know in Matthew where it says go and make disciples of all nations? It doesn't say go when your children are out of the house and they are all grown up, or when your bills are paid, your house is all in order, or you feel good. He said go and he meant now!" She closed her testimonial by saying, "When you are in the storms of life, just go, listen to God and go, he has me in his hands he has you in his hands."

If the Bethehope website is not complete, contact me at rodk@ bethehope.net for information about scheduling me for speaking. Contact me for information about any of the other facets of the Bethehope Rainbow! The rainbow has 7 colors. If you include my book, the Bethehope Rainbow vision has 7 facets!

My prayer for all who have joined Beth and I on our journey is to truly experience the words of Romans 15:13, "May the God of hope fill you with all joy and peace as you trust in Him so that you may overflow with hope by the power of the Holy Spirit!"